INDIA HERE I COME…THERE I GO

Ninety visits to India

MAURICE HARVEY

ISBN 978-1-78792-116-0

All photographs by the author.

Book design, layout and production management by Into Print
www.intoprint.net
+44 (0)1604 832149

My thanks to Mark Webb and his team, and to Brian Watcher for helpful advice.

Second edition, revised 2026

Dedicated to

To my faithful family, Lorraine, Rosanne and Clive, who at the time of my travels, kept the home fires burning during my many trips abroad to many strange places when there were no emails or texts, WhatsApp or Viber, Facebook or Cell phones, Instagram or Twitter.

Also by Maurice Harvey

*Shooting the Globe**
Reading the Funny Bible and Other Stories
Romancing Remy – Aunty to OFWs
OFWs Modern Day Heroes
Into the Great Unknown
Blown up by the Bible
They Called me Their Daughter
No Protocol for Me
Pagsinta Kay Remy

Written in conjunction with Lorraine Harvey
Light for Life

*Winner of the Daystar Award for the best book of its genre.

Contents

PREFACE

When I consider the vastness and complexity of India, I wonder at myself attempting to write about this great nation. But this is not a description, a travel guide or critique of India, but simply my personal experiences of many visits to a country that has become the most populous on earth.

> The most important thing to understand about India is its complexity. "There never was a land so riddled by inconsistency, so defiant of generalisation, so bewilderingly varied, or so preposterously loaded with idiosyncrasies. It is doubtful whether anyone has ever understood more than a few parts of it well, and none, certainly, can have comprehended it all, for the full range of India is too wide and too elusive and too detailed to grasp."
> *Rail Across India,* Paul C. Pet, Geoffrey Moorhouse, Brian Hollingsworth, Abbeville Publishers.

As one pastor said to me, 'We have the best of the best, and the worst of the worst.'

It is possible to say almost anything about India and have it apply to some part of that subcontinent. It is a nation both powerful and weak, ancient and modern, rich and poor.

For ten years I was the distribution consultant to the Bible Society in India, then twenty years the official photojournalist of the United Bible Societies – the world's largest publisher. I wrote about and photographed their work in India plus 161 other countries.

Then I gave five years as the North and South Asia director of the American child sponsorship programme Compassion International. As a sideline I was the Asia correspondent of the *International Railway Journal.*

These varied duties took me to all parts of India except Goa, Darjeeling, the Andaman Islands and a few states in the North East which were forbidden to foreigners. Every visit leaving me excited to be there, then after two or three weeks, glad to be going home again.

CHAPTER ONE

BOMBAY-MUMBAI

My sixteen passports were scattered all over the table. The kids had been playing with them. 'Gosh dad, look at all those funny stamps! Some are just blotches and I can't read them, others take a full page. Here's a funny one it says, "to go."'

'No, that's Togo. It's a tiny country in West Africa.

'Here's another one, it says "be in." It takes up a full page.'

'Oh, that's another tiny country in West Africa called Benin.'

'I keep on seeing India. Lots of them.'

'That's funny. Such small stamps for such a big country.'

'Let's count them.' They found about 90.

Every country of the world is changing all the time and none more so than India. The India I knew has completely changed in the past twenty-five years. Like one fellow who said, 'Even the rickshaw wallah has a cell phone now.'

The descriptions I give can be considered historical rather than a travel guide for today as they date from 1960 to 2001 and the changes since then have been immense. The country was in a sad state the last time I was there. A local writer published a book in 2000 in which he declared the shameful condition of his country.[1] The lives of so many had not improved after 53 years of independence when the population stood at 350,000,000. But now has become the most populous place on earth. The average per capita income was $450 placed 162nd out of 206 countries. At that time half the population lived on one dollar per person a day. Seventy-one percent did not have access to sanitation and life expectancy was 63 years and infant mortality was tragically high. Four out of ten men were illiterate and the rate higher among women. There were also 1.78 million graduates in the year 2000.

However tremendous gains have been made in the last twenty five years with the country becoming a major player on the world

---

1 Gurcharan Das, *India Unbound*, Penguin Books.

scene. Take literacy. This grew from 18 percent in 1951, to 74 percent in 2011. The population has now grown to 1,465,000,000.

Thomas Friedman in his book *The World is Flat*[2] makes a fascinating comparison between Christopher Columbus and himself.

> "Columbus was searching for hardware – precious metals, silk and spices – the sources of wealth in his day. I was searching for software, brain power, complex algorithms, knowledge workers, call centres, transmission protocols, breakthroughs in optical engineering – the sources of wealth of our day. He called the people he discovered 'Indians,' and their country 'the Indies.' He had accidently ran into America but thought he had discovered part of India. I actually found India and thought that many of the people there were Americans. Some had taken American names, and others were doing great imitations of American accents at call centres and American business techniques and software labs."

One of the regular trials that citizens of the USA face each year is their tax returns. I've heard many American friends complain about this. But now-a-days, they can have them done by an Indian accountant who might be a housewife working from her kitchen table in a rural village in North India. The number doing this has risen from 25,000 in 2003 to 100,000 a year later.

But I could see changes coming. Many young people passing out of schools speaking English, and regardless of their caste, have succeeded gaining employment in growing industries. I was often in Bangalore, now Bengaluru, where the Bible Society of India has its head office. This city had long been a centre for composing and printing books. Hundreds of Bibles in different languages were composed here and sent away to another country like Hong Kong or South Korea for printing. When computerisation began to appear, it was a short step from hand-composing to utilising the computer.

The internet has opened enormous opportunities. My nephew, Brian Harvey, an aerial photographer in Australia, would photograph a large area of the country such as every metre of an entire railway line hundreds of kilometres long in Western Australia, then

---

2 Thomas Friedman, *The World is Flat*, Penguin Books.

send the electronic files to a photographic business in India. They would make a print many metres long of the line at about 10% of the cost of having it done in Australia and take only a couple of days to do it. The railway management would then be able to examine every detail of the line to ensure everything was intact thus making a huge saving on not having to inspect it visually.

By 1960 the huge number of educated young people were having an impact on the world in many cases without leaving home. A radiologist in England can send his x-rays to a specialist in India for a report and have it back within hours. I met an American gynaecologist on a plane, and he told me that when he needed a second opinion, he simply photographed the details of his patient's problem with his cell phone and emailed the pictures to a specialist in New Delhi. A few hours later he would have it.

There was a new industry developing, known as Call Centres specially in Bangalore, a city I knew. There I came across dozens of young people in coffee shops and restaurants eating and drinking in a way their parents would never dreamed have of doing. We have all had the experience of talking to someone about our telephone bill, a delayed courier package or asking for help with a bank password and wondering about the accent of the person we were dealing with! It possibly was someone in a call centre in Bangalore or New Delhi.

Finding jobs for all the millions of school leavers each year is an enormous headache for the government. According to the Centre for Monitoring the Indian Economy (CMIE), which provides regular data on unemployment, the urban unemployment rate was 10.08 per cent in June last year. In the academic year 2020, 17,000,000 students graduated in every discipline imaginable.[3] The 2020 population was estimated at 1,380,004,385 at mid-year according to UN data. So 10% of that figure is about 13,800,000 unemployed. Statistics *Wikipedia.*

---

3 All India Survey of Higher Education (AISHE).

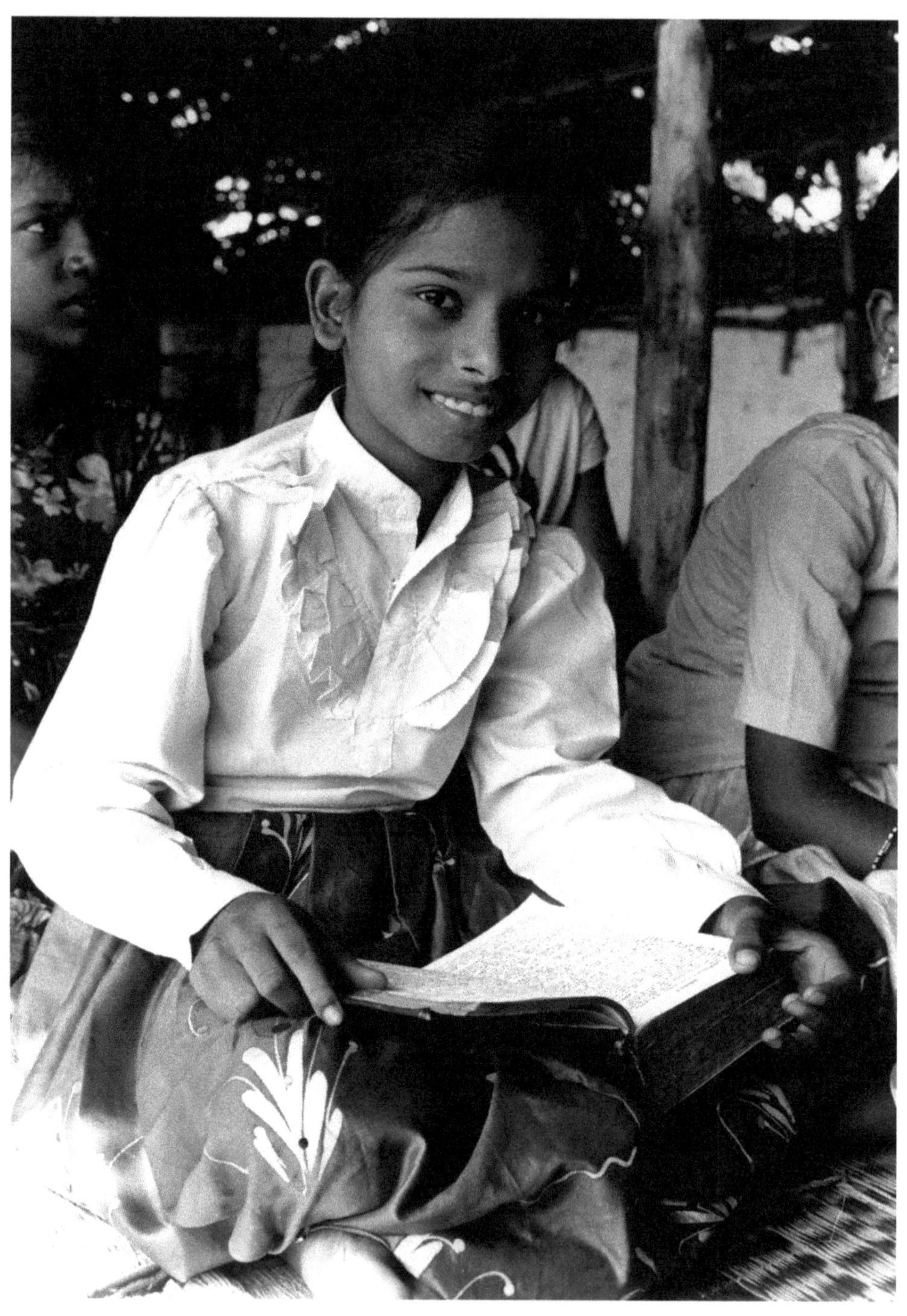

School girl, Kerela.
We wouldn't consider a typist without a degree.

A report by Deloitte quoting (ASHE) shows, as at October 2021, the student enrolment in higher education in India as 34.3 million, with male and female equally divided. *Wikipedia.*

Indian Railways is the largest employer in the nation. When the Danapur Division decided on a major employment programme in 2021, they advertised 35,000 vacancies. But they were swamped with 100,000,000 (yes, that's millions!) applications.

When the COVID-19 virus struck, the World Health Organisation asked India for their statistics of cases. I heard a doctor in New Delhi saying on the BBC World Service, 'How can we possibly know how many there are? We have about 240,000 medical centres in the 600,000 villages in villages throughout India, how can they all suddenly communicate with us over a period of a few days? Can you imagine, our office getting 240,000 texts with their information? How many people would we need to deal with them! 'The official estimates give a total 43,000,000 cases with 522,000 deaths but I think it could be as much as a hundred times more than that!'

My first time there was when I spent a week in Bombay, now Mumbai, on my way to Africa in 1960. At that time the cheapest way to Northern Rhodesia (now Zambia) from New Zealand, was by sea via Sydney, Ceylon, Bombay, Seychelles, Mombasa, Beira, and Bulawayo, changing boats three times and trains twice. It took 54 days but now it can be done in about 24 hours. The following is my description of my first visit taken from my book *Into the Great Unknown*.[4]

> At noon the next day we arrived in Bombay. As we moved slowly against the wharf I could see scores, actually it seemed like hundreds, of uniformed coolies all yelling for business. As soon as the gangway was down they rushed on board and I was surrounded by a dozen grinning, yelling men pleading for work. I chose seven of them. The luggage had been brought out of the baggage room and stacked up on the deck. It was not a little disconcerting to see how my bright green tin trunks, each one weighing about 30kg was snatched up, placed on the heads of the porters who quickly left the ship. I watched the trunks bobbing up and down in the sea of

4 *Into the Great Unknown*. iUniverse.

black heads of the people on the wharf and wondered if I would ever see it again.

I took my turn at customs and immigration who came on board to check us out, and was soon down on the wharf, where New Zealand missionary Harold McGregor, was waiting to receive me. He led me to the customs shed and behold, there were my trunks neatly piled up, with seven smiling porters holding out their hands for their fee.

The MacGregors had a typical Bombay apartment, with a flat roof painted with a yellow wash, in the suburb of Bandra. On arrival, we sat down to drink several cups of tea, 'we don't count them' said Harold, and then set off to the market. We purchased some cloth and took it to a tailor who made up a suit and some shorts for me within a couple of days.

I had a seven-day stay in Bombay and had my first experience of working with an interpreter while I preached. I was invited to speak at several church services and Bible studies. One day, I spoke at an open-air meeting in Bandra bazaar where we had an audience of over 200 people all of whom stood quietly and attentively. My message was interpreted into the local language, Marathi. Harold said that I 'spoke like a professional as though I had been doing this all my life.'

I already knew a little about Bombay from the stories my father had told about the place. He had worked at sea as a young man and served in the merchant navy during the First World War. It was when his steam ship was replenishing its coal supplies in Bombay that he heard that he had become a father for the first time. I had always entertained a secret wish to visit the place one day. My father would tell us of the way hundreds of coolies would file aboard, each with a basket of coal on his head and tip it into the coal bunker. There were two gangplanks – one up and one down. The coal was usually quite fine and very dusty. As a result, the dust would rise out of the bunker, enveloping everything and everyone. The coaling went on continuously throughout the night until the bunkers were full. On completion, the ship was in a filthy condition with coal dust everywhere. It is still the world's third largest coal producer.

What really amazed me about Bombay, were the countless numbers of people. I had just come from a country with a total population of just over four million. So many living in huts and shacks made of every type of material imaginable, many in a wretched condition. But I soon learned that the poor shacks made of bits of tin, plastic and wood, were not necessarily a sign of poverty. There was such a shortage of housing that many people had to resort to makeshift dwellings. From these simple huts emerged men, women and children dressed in spotless white clothes beautifully laundered and ironed as they set off to work and school. There are, however, large areas of slums.

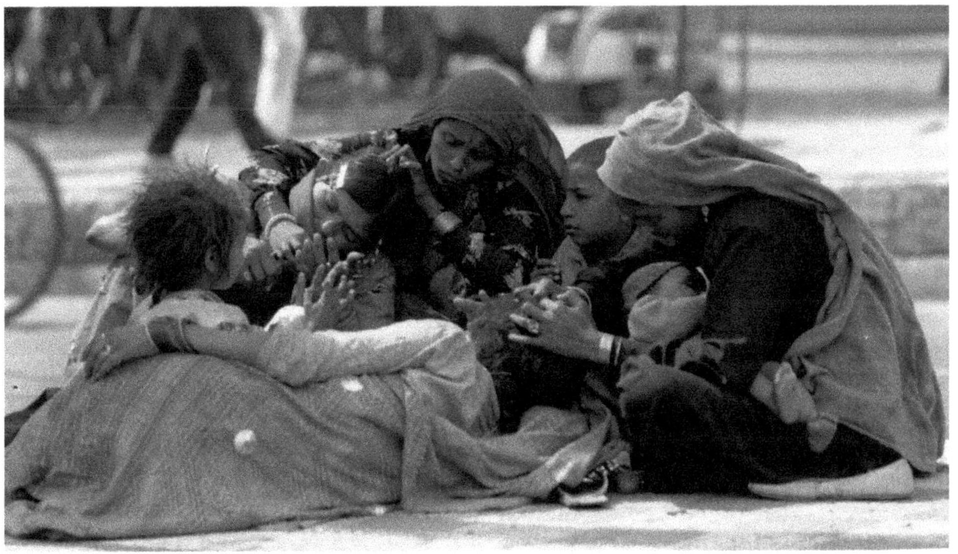

Women and children helping each with hair care. Bombay.

Bombay was known to the Portuguese, back in 1538, when they called it Bom Bahia, Portuguese for 'Good Bay.' Mumbai, it's present name, is from the Hindu religion. Ptolemy the Greek astronomer and geographer in AD150 called it Heptansia – the city of seven islands, so back then it must have been a significant place. These island are now joined together by causeways and bridges making them indistinguishable from each other.

In 1549 the islands of Bombay were handed over in perpetuity to Garcia da Orta for a yearly rent of 85 pounds sterling. In 1625 an Anglo Dutch fleet captured Bombay fort and looted the island and left suddenly.

On 23 June 1661 king Charles II of England married princess Catherine de Braganza of Portugal and the island of Bombay was given in dowry to king Charles by an alliance of marriage. Then 1688 it was handed over to the East India company.[5]

In an effort to return to its roots, Bombayites decided to change the name of their great city to Mumbai, So now it's residents are called Mumbaikars or Mumbians. One reason was to be rid of names from the time of the British Raj but to many people, this was a joke, because it was the name the first European colonisers gave it – the Portuguese.

Another day I went to town on my own and had a great time at the bazaar. The quantity of the things on sale was overwhelming. As my diary records:

> A walk around the Bandra bazaar was a real experience – the yelling of meat vendors as they cheerfully patted slim joints of goat and mutton urging me to buy, the flies, the smells of the fish market and the beefy smell of the beef market. These enterprising 'butchers' had about a four-foot section of the bench and sat in the middle of their piles of meat. It was not laid out according to the way we cut up a carcase, but simply chopped up into small pieces. Roast whole leg of lamb was apparently not included in Indian cuisine. Cows and pigs wandered around along with mangy scabby dogs.
>
> The next day I caught the train into the city where I spent a long time in Crawford Market and bought a few clothes and a suitcase. This was the same train as a crowd of men who were taking lunch to people working in the city. The meal is packed in a tin container with several layers with the address painted on the lid. There are several thousand of these men known as *tiffin wallahs.* A friendly gent on the train seated next to me explained the history of these men. Later, back at the railway station, I opened my new case to put something away, and a large crowd of people immediately gathered around to see what was inside! A tout approached me and asked if I had seen Crawford Road yet. No, only Crawford market. 'Ah, but you must

5 Harish Booch, *Pocket Bombay Guide*, Lakhani Book Depot, 1982.

see the Crawford Road and see the girls in their cages.' I had never heard of this unfortunate tourist attraction and fortunately declined. Later I learned that this is where young women prostitutes who come from all over India and Nepal are held under guard, and Harold very gravely said, 'that was wise not to go there.'

As I took in all the suffering and poverty, the beggars, people bathing, eating and sleeping on the streets, the blind and lame, tiny babies lying naked asleep on dirty footpaths, the gabble of a strange language, I was thankful I didn't have to stay in India. I watched a man with neither fingers nor toes rolling through mud in an effort to attract attention and gain a few coins. When I arrived back at the McGregor's' apartment, Harold was astounded and a little angry that I had bought the suitcase, telling me that it would have been so easy to be cheated. He was even more surprised when I told him that I had paid only 30 Rupees for it. The price had started at 300! He sat down and muttered, 'Well I suppose you'll do all right in Africa,' which I took to mean that I knew how to look after myself in a foreign culture.

The Bombay suburban trains deserve a mention. I was advised to go into the city after the morning rush hour. The 10.00 a.m. train was densely crowded but, I was told, at 8.00 a.m. it would only be jam-packed. I went back to the station next morning just to see how packed the trains really were. Every carriage had four doors on either side, and there were usually six to eight men hanging on to and out of each doorway, well beyond the profile of the carriage. Some passengers were riding the buffers between the carriages. There were so many people on the roofs of the trains that I couldn't count them – all riding perilously close to overhead wires that carried 1,500 volts DC. Remember this was 1960 and those days of roof-riding commuters are no longer can be seen in Bombay.

Here's a quote from a recent article that shows the situation hasn't changed that much:

'The current problem of over-crowding is so grave, and the pressure on the infrastructure and facilities so high, that 4,700 passengers are packed into a 9-rake (nine carriages) during peak hours, as against the rated capacity of 1,700. It is now not uncommon to see 14 to 16 passengers per square meter of floor space, causing what is known as 'super dense crush' load. In other words, 550 people crammed into a carriage built to carry 200.

There are approximately 3,500 deaths on the Mumbai suburban system every year – that's more than 9 every day! Many of these deaths are caused by people attempting to cross the railway tracks on foot, avoiding the overhead bridges that are provided for their use. Not a few get swiped off from hanging outside the profile of the carriage. When a fatality is reported that part of the line is closed for a few minutes until it is cleared, then opened again. Compare that to Auckland where if there was an incident like that, they close down the whole system for an hour or two while the police and security people photograph and measure the scene.

As well as being a UNESCO World Heritage Site, every day over 1,250 local and long-distance trains pull in and out of Victoria Station's 18 platforms. This is a magnificent building built in 1888 and named after Queen Victoria. But in 1996, the Minister of Railways, changed the name of the station to Chhatrapati Shivaji Terminus.

About three million passengers pass through it every day – that's more people than travel on the entire British railway network per day. The 'super dense crush load' of the commuter network's peak times is no exaggeration – up to 5000 passengers cram themselves into trains built to hold only 1200.[6]

The trains are usually so crowded that the Western Railway permits them to depart up to 3 minutes before the scheduled departure at en route stations. At 'super dense crush load,' there's no point in waiting for more passengers! However, at originating stations train will leave only at scheduled departure time

I took many photographs, which was not easy because of the way people would crowd around wanting to get in the photo. Later that day, the tailor called me to come and collect my new clothes. One suit, three pairs of trousers and two pairs of shorts cost me nine

---

6 Open University.

pounds Sterling. After six days, my ship for East Africa was ready to sail.

I loved going to India, but I was equally glad to be back home again. It's a land of such great contrasts – having the best of the best and worst of the worst. I met people from both extremes – from a poor widow living under a single sheet of old rusty corrugated iron propped up against a tree and who owned one sari, a cooking pot, and a large knife, to the scion of a rich landowner in Calcutta, who lived in a huge palace with over 200 servants. (He actually didn't know the exact number!)

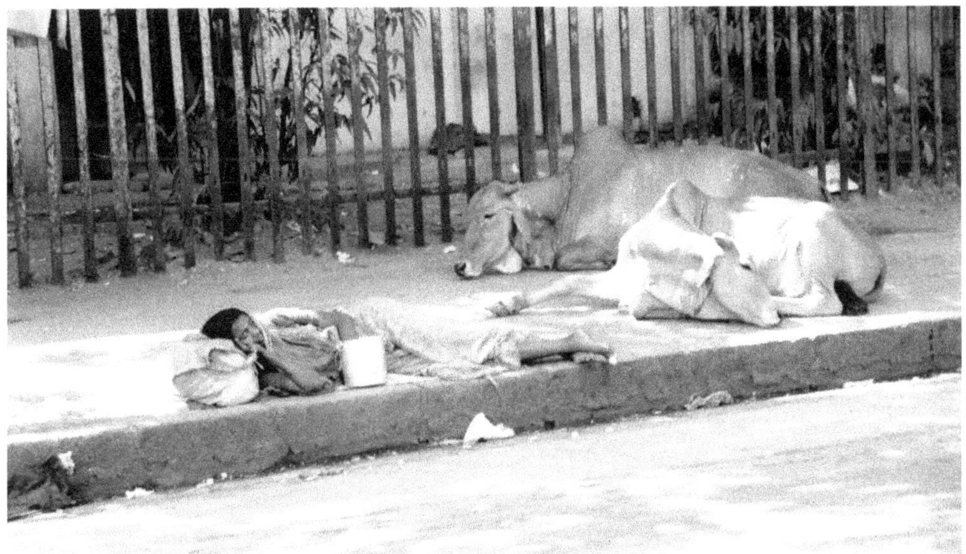

At rest, Bombay.

CHAPTER TWO

TRAIN TO AGRA

I was visiting Delhi with my colleague Antony Harrop when we decided to visit Agra and in particular see the Taj Mahal. The Janata Express ran the 200 kilometres between Delhi and Agra and was still hauled by a steam locomotive.

Before departure I went to see the locomotive and have a chat with the crew. It was relatively new as far as steam engines go as it was only 15 years since built in India. The oldest working steam locomotive in India is 164 years old. The driver on learning that I was a former steam loco man invited me to travel on the footplate between the second and third stops. This I did and asked if I could bring my colleague up on the return journey. He readily agreed so long as I warned him of the danger etc like showing him where to stand saying, 'don't move from here and hang on tightly.'

The station master came up and had a few words with the driver handing him the key, which was the permission to run to the next station, what we called a tablet in New Zealand. The fireman opened the firebox door to reveal the fire that was a mass of violet flames and exceedingly hot and in perfect condition. That colour indicated that the coal had burnt through and when more coal was added it would immediately begin to burn. We were ready to go. The steam pressure was just a touch under 210 lbs per square inch. Antony was aghast at it's heat.

The rightaway was given and the driver tugged the whistle cord above his head, just a brief pop, and we were away. He then eased open the regulator. This is usually a long lever so that he could open it firmly but gently as it was moving a valve against the steam pressure. Steam began to emerge from the cylinders with a loud hiss as it drained the water that would have been accumulated while it was standing still. If he didn't allow the water to escape the piston would have blown the end off the cylinder because water cannot be compressed. From the chimney came the usual blast and we began to move.

The platform beside began to move, at least that's what it felt like to my friend as the engine began to move so gently.

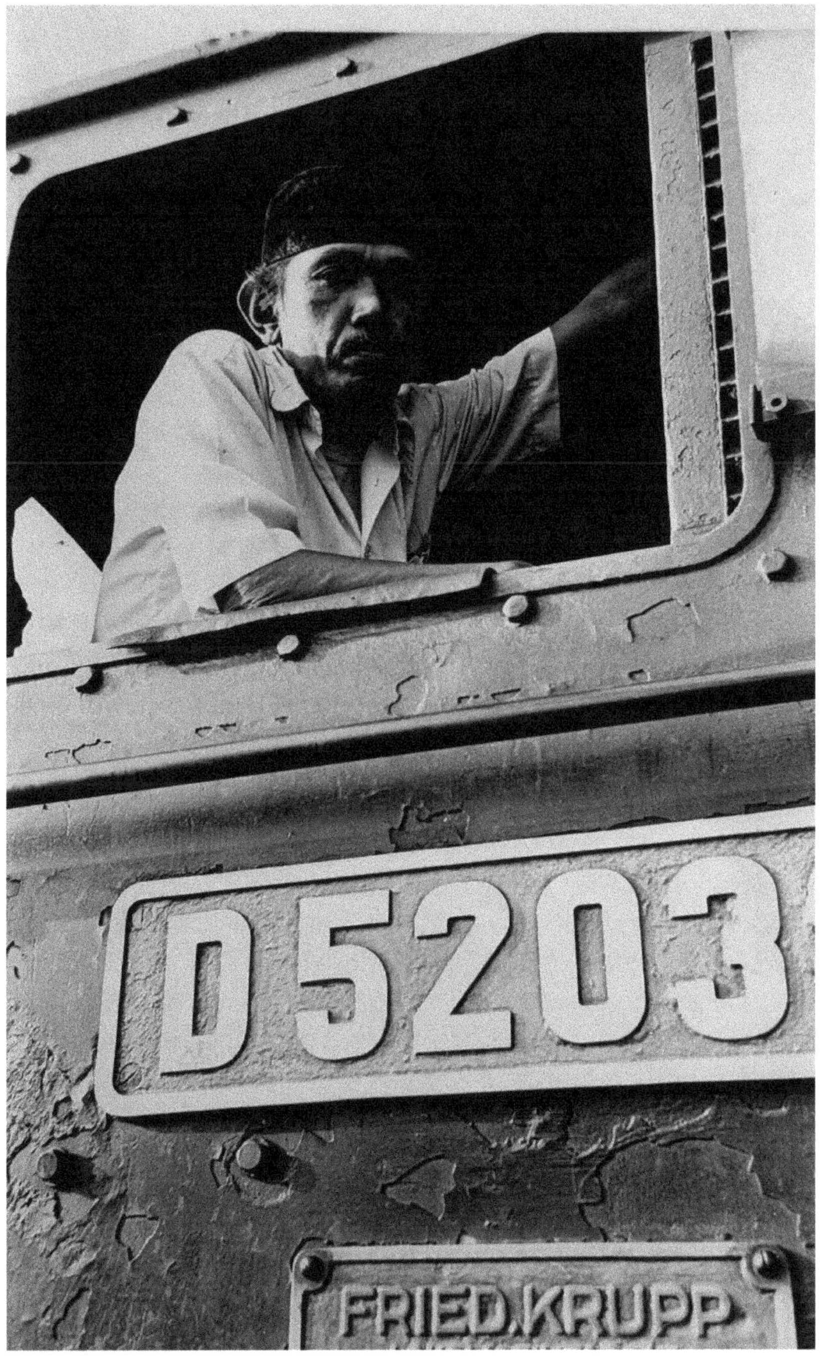

Engine driver, Indian Railways.

My friend was amazed at the noise and vibration as we slowly pulled out of the station and I'll never forget the look on his face as we slowly gathered speed. The driver spun the reversing wheel that shortened the cut-off of the stroke to the cylinders. The noise grew louder and louder and the footplate began to move from side to side. His expression seemed to be saying 'It can't get louder than this, it can't go any faster.' But it did! The W.P. loco No 7116 was India's best and ran, with a standard passenger trins at 110 kph – at least that was the regulation speed but it obviously could attain a much faster speed. Later in the trip, I noticed we were running at about 140kph.

Slowly we moved away from the platform and threaded our way through the mass of tracks ahead and we were soon out of the city. Among the many signals were a couple at green so that was the way we would go.

The driver had the luxury of two firemen, and stripped to the waist, one put on the first fire. That's railway speak of putting coal on the fire. The second fireman's job was to was to keep dragging the coal forward to within easy reach. As the steam exhausted out of the chimney it draws air, i.e. oxygen through the firebox. The fire that was simply a spread of violet flames soon became a roaring mass of white-hot heat at about 2500C. The fireman skilfully fired in a dozen shovelfuls of coal neatly spreading it evenly all over the fire. The coal was rather poor quality with a high ash content so needed careful handling in the large firebox that measured 46 square feet. He knew his work and understood that type of coal he had for that trip and kept a perfect fire all the way to Agra. The tender carried 5,000 gallons of water and 20 tons of coal.

The coal began to burn immediately, and this was evidenced by the black smoke that poured from the chimney. I admired his skill in turning the shovel over to spread the coal evenly. That took a lot of practise. Many years later Antony confessed that it was one his most memorable experiences in India.

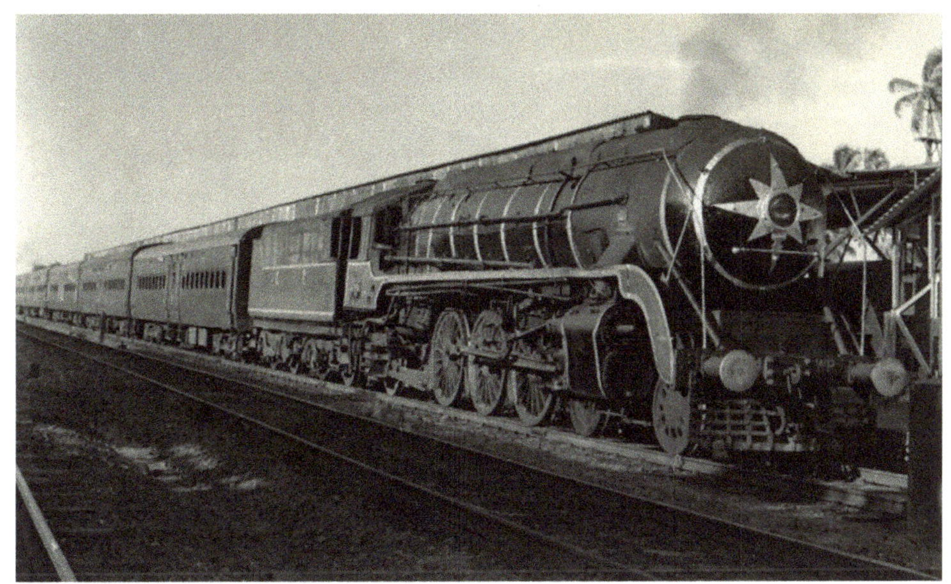

Delhi-Agra Express, Indian Railways.

I had many trips on the footplate of steam engines in India. There was always a warm welcome from the crew when they found out of my personal railway experience. One time, north of Calcutta there were children playing on the line ahead. The driver didn't even whistle to warn them. All he said was 'they will get off when they see us.' Later on the same trip, there were a couple of goats on the line, he whistled and whistled to scare them off. 'They would derail us if we hit them.'

A colleague Russell Self who had worked in India for many years had advised me to visit the Taj Mahal at the first opportunity. 'You haven't seen India, until you've seen the Taj.' It truly is a wonderful spectacle. Built by the Mughal ruler Shah Jahan in memory of his beloved wife, it is the most famous building in the country and took 22 years to build. His favourite wife was quite a woman. She bore him 14 children in 17 years of marriage but died in childbirth. His full name was A'la Azad Abul Muzaffar Shahab ud-Din Mohammad Shah Jahan.

Over the years I visited this tomb about six times. I saw it in all kinds of weather and light. No matter climatic conditions or the time of day or night, it is the most beautiful building you could wish to see. Dazzling white in the sunshine or ghostly in the night.

The sad part of the story is that the Shah had planned his own tomb to be like a negative image to his wife's built of black marble. But his son became fed up with his father's spending and took over the throne. He imprisoned his father in the Red Fort across the Yamuna River. From there he spent the rest of his life gazing at his beloved's tomb.

There is another magnificent building in Agra built for another 'ravishingly beautiful woman, Mehru-un Nissa.' Emperor Jahangir saw her at the annual fair. He married her and called her the Light of the World (Nur Jahan) and raised her father to the highest position in his court. When he died the daughter built a mausoleum to his memory. The craftsmen surpassed themselves with a profusion of intricate chikan-work or embroidery, translucent marble screens inlay work of precious stones.

In another building called the Agra Fort, there is a special bathroom that is lined with hundreds of small mirrors. The flame of a single small lamp lit in there is reflected countless times.

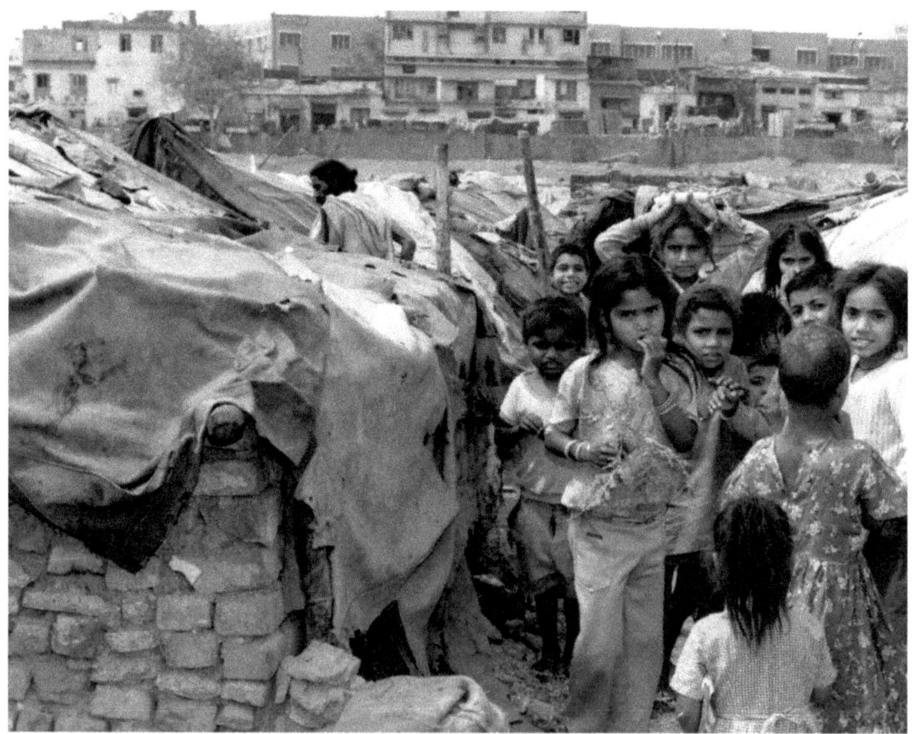

Children, Delhi slums.

CHAPTER THREE

DELHI

One morning as I came to the front door of my Delhi hotel, a rickshaw driver asked me where I wanted to go. I had no immediate plans and answered, 'Nowhere.'

'Ah then I will take you somewhere, somewhere very good. Do you know the spice market? Its the largest in the world. Come get in, I will take you.' He continued to chat and after discovering that I was from New Zealand, he shouted, 'That's wonderful. I took Walter Hadlee in this my rickshaw. He's a great cricketer.'

He was clearly excited to have customer as he wove his way between lanes of vehicles spewing exhaust into the grimy air. I pointed to a slum area but he refused to take me there. The aroma of the spices was almost overpowering as we approached the market called Khari Baoli. It was mass of colour. There was every shade of red, orange and yellow. One writer in Wikipedia described this market as 'one of the spiciest countries in the world is home to Asia's largest spice market. New Delhi's Khari Baoli dates back to the 17th century, and a visit there will take you on a kaleidoscopic adventure of the most colourful spices.' The air pollution was bad that day and it was growing worse year after year. Even now as I write this, the news from Delhi tells of schools being closed for days. The government is desperately trying to find ways to clean up the air of the capital city.

The spice market in Delhi can trace its origins back to 1650, when it was built by one of the five wives of Mughal emperor Shah Jahan. (He built the Taj Mahal.) It grew to become the largest spice market in Asia. I was told that some stalls are run by tenth, eleventh or even twelfth-generation storeowners. That sounded like an exaggeration but I got the meaning. Like any Asian spice market, Khari Baoli is a 'smorgasbord for the senses.' The spices are of every colour of every shade and hue imaginable, a kaleidoscope of colour. The air was thick with saffron and cumin. Along with the spices there is a great variety of dried fruits, herbs, nuts, teas, grains, rice and pasta.

When we stopped at a traffic light, an elderly man leant against the motor rickshaw and thrust the stump of his arm through the window and brandished it in my face. He had no teeth and gabbled something in Hindi. It sounded like *'mujhe paise do,'* – give me money. Paise was money, and that's what he was asking for. This was yet another image of poverty and suffering that plagues the mind of a visitor to this country. Suddenly the rickshaw took off trying to beat all the other traffic across the intersection. This was my first day back in India and I was quickly becoming accustomed to the frenetic activity of the traffic. But I couldn't help but admire the skill of my driver as he slammed on the brakes to avoid a bus that cut into our lane then lurched around it narrowly missing a dilapidated truck albeit painted a bright orange and red that came at us on the other side. Suddenly it seemed that there was no room for us but somehow our rickshaw slid into a space that hadn't existed moments ago.

The market was crowded with every type of person imaginable. Housewives carefully selecting their spices that made them the greatest of cooks. I never had a poor meal in an Indian home. But as one lady said, 'It's our curries and spices that make us great.' I spoke to one distinguished gentleman and asked him if he was a chef. 'Oh no,' he said, 'My wife does all the cooking but she uses only what I buy.'

'Doesn't she sometimes come to see what is offering.'

'Certainly not. She cooks for me!'

That was an interesting insight into that marital relationship.

There many touts offering to guide me, beggars, tourists, guides and pick pockets, and one horrible-looking man whispered, 'I have a young woman for you, or a boy. They are new and clean that will please your good self.' Even to my untrained eye, I could see a number of young fellows who were obviously offering drugs. Then to cheer me up considerably, a young couple offered to sell me *a Good News Bible*. I checked the publishing details. It was a copy of one of the editions I had personally had a hand in it's publication. It was a relatively new translation especially designed for people who speak English as a second language. I had personally ordered 50,000 copies for India, and there I was, with one in my hand.

One of the men who attended a Scripture distribution workshop in New Delhi, in which I described how the Scriptures could be used in evangelism, was an South East Asian man. I was intrigued that he was there and invited him to eat with me one evening. He was a member of the embassy staff and also served the pastor of a church that served the Filipino community in Delhi. It was surprising to hear that, as well as the diplomatic staff, there were quite a number of Filipino people employed as house maids, nannies, chefs and carers. 'They are all away from home,' he said, 'and as such need a counsellor and friend outside of their work. Some of them are troubled people looking for a new life, but usually they can't leave their problems behind.' At that time, it was quite a fashionable thing to have, in this land of servants, one from the Philippines.

One of the group was a young woman who stood up to tell us her story. 'One day, I saw a lady selling small packets of books. There was one in my language so I bought it for only five rupees. That night I put aside my study books and read these things I had bought. They were Christian. At first I was annoyed with myself for wasting five rupees on such rubbish. But as I read the little book called *Mark,* I began to realise that I didn't really know anything about the Christian religion or gods. I applied for the free Bible correspondence course that was advertised and a few days later received a very nice letter from a lady who offered to meet and help me to understand the faith. Incredibly she lived in the same street as me. Within a couple of days, I decided to become a Christian. This moved me further away from my family, all of whom were fanatical Hindus. I dared not tell them about my conversion as they are likely to kill me. I knew this because I had heard of them doing that to other people. But the pastor tells me that I should do that, so one day I will go and see them.'

CHAPTER FOUR

HOLI AND HIPPIES

A few days later was the Holi festival. This is a Hindu festival celebrating the victory of good over evil and the eternal love of Radha and Krishna, and the beginning of spring. Although this was a festival that people enjoyed including the tourists, but it was something I wished to avoid. The people celebrate this Hindu festival of colours, by smearing each other with powders of every colour imaginable, like red, green, blue and pink and dousing each other with water. They dance, and share slops and drink with family and friends.

This colourful time is not for photographers with expensive camera gear. Those in the know will use a simple cheap one that will get plastered with coloured powder that will be very difficult to remove.

Holi marks the arrival of spring in India, Nepal and other South Asian countries. I was in Burma one year and got caught. It celebrates the divine love between gods and is a time of rebirth and rejuvenation, embracing the positive and letting go of negative energy.

One has to be careful where you go as there could be people throwing balloons of coloured water from balconies. People using water pistols should be avoided.

But everywhere there are people offering each other, including tourists, all kinds of food and drink. But if you aren't into drugs its best to avoid cakes and chocolate laced with what they call bhang. But the people of all ages covered in brightly coloured powder make for great photos.

The Bible Society of India usually held its annual staff conference in one of the 17 sates of the country. I was invited to one held in the north eastern state of Meghalaya which is one of few Christian-majority states in India. On the Sunday morning one of the church leaders heard that we were there and he decided that we should have a public meeting for all churches. He put out the word that morning and astonishly, in the afternoon, about 5,000 people gathered to meet us.

We were greatly honoured to be accommodated in the rooms of the Legislative Council. It was very cold and there were coal fire places and stoves in every room of the building, but, because winter had not officially started they were not lit. There were cold draughts through the cracks in the wall so we blocked them with newspapers. After two days all the fires were lit. The staff had faithfully followed the rule that no fires could be lit until the official start of winter.

The place that held the world record for the most rain was only a few kilometres away so took a bus trip there. This was Cherrapunji. It receives the highest rainfall in India. It is reportedly the wettest place on Earth, with an average annual rainfall of 11,872 millimetres (467.4 in). According to the Guinness Book of World Records, Mawsynram a village nearby, received 26,000 millimetres (1,000 in) of rainfall in 1985. (Wikipedia) But local people of Cherrapunji said that their place was the wettest getting 500 inches per annum and a world record was set in 1886 of 905 inches. But it was a fine dry afternoon when we visited.

HIPPIES

One of the deeply distressing sights was the numbers of European young people who had come to India to 'find themselves.' Dressing and trying and look like Hindu Indians, many of them immersed themselves into what they thought was an experience that would raise them to a higher spiritual level like spending time in an ashram to learn from a self-appointed guru, trying to gain a more meaningful connection with themselves. Some of them, from their appearances, seem to believe that the grubbier their clothes and bodies became, the holier they would get! There were many who crept home laden with hepatitis or some tropical bug, deeply disappointed with the 'spiritual' experience. I chatted with many, maybe hundreds, and never met anyone who had realised their dreams.

Travelling on a train one day I greeted a young European woman and sat opposite her. She shyly returned my greeting but after about 30 minutes, she looked up and said, "Can we chat?" I agreed and she began to tell me about her time in India. Clearly, she was anxious to tell someone about her experience in an ashram, or, as she put it, "Some of those gurus are so unholy. They are just businessmen making as much money as possible." Coming to India to 'find herself' had proved disastrous. She explained how she had done as much research as possible and found one that looked very good for her needs. This was a small ashram in a jungle area in Gujarat that she was told about. It was said to be quite exclusive in that you had to apply to stay there. Not like so many others where you just walk in, pay your money, and make yourself at home. It was necessary to apply online and pay a month's board and lodging in advance with your credit card and wait for an invitation. It was expensive too, over fifty pounds a day and that's as much as ten times others charge. There was no refund if you only stayed a week. The answer came the next day and it simply said, 'Come and bring just yourself and nothing else.'

On arrival at the ashram, she was interviewed by two English women who demanded that she surrender all items of make-up and clothing except a hairbrush, and dress in a simple sari, no blouse, or underclothes. They explained that the message saying bring just yourself meant just that. They said, 'While you are here, you must empty yourself of everything so that the guru's teaching can fill you.' The teaching began that day, a long boring discourse that she found difficult to understand. It wasn't just his accent, but long descriptions of the gods.

There were about thirty 'pilgrims' as they were called, who came from all over the world. There was one large room that served as a dining room and a dormitory bedroom. We all slept together, men and women. 'It was wonderful how everyone respected each other and there was no hanky panky at nights.' As time went by the teaching became more understandable. Three girls from Bali, who were on leave from their cruise ship, offered free massages, not the tradition Ayurvedic but their own Balinese style.

Two Japanese lady doctors gave private tuition to us ladies teaching good hygiene, eating and living practises. 'It was a lovely group of people, sincerely trying to find the meaning of life. The best times were eating together and discussing the teaching. They tell me that in most ashrams eating must be done in silence because some gurus say that eating is filling your body that now belongs to the gods, so you worship them as you eat. The guru said that everything you do is like worshipping the gods, be it eating, walking, making love, counting your money or bathing. But this guru kept on referring to money and sex. I only went to one ashram, but I met some people who spend all their time going from one to the other for months on end. They all have different rules, and I was lucky in the sense that I found one that was very easy going and didn't force people to follow all their worship and praying that was going on all the time. Their first session was before dawn but that was too early for me so I never attended it. One couple told me that they had spent six months staying in ashrams, usually a month at a time. Everywhere the food was good but in this one, it was exceptional. The curries ranged from very mild to extremely hot meal was quite delicious.

One evening, a helper came to me and quietly told me to follow her as the guru wanted to see me. He hardly ever talked to any of us individually and I was told that it was a great honour to be called to him. I was told that as soon as I entered his room, to sit down on the floor by the door and wait for him to call me. I did that but he immediately beckoned me to approach him. He was seated on several layers of cloth and quilts that were his bed. The room was richly decorated with hanging drapes and Persian rugs. In one corner was a huge grandfather clock but no other furniture except a large wardrobe.

"Come and sit by me and tell me all about yourself," he said. "Have you reached Moksa yet? You know what that is don't you? Its eternal and blessed peace." In fact, the other day he talked about that for two hours and didn't leave me any the wiser.

'As I talked, he held my hands and rubbed up and down my arms. Oh, sorry, I can't tell you anything else because he raped me. He said that it helped him to worship god and at the climax he touched god. When he discovered I was a virgin he shouted, "Ram. Ram, or god, god.'

'I was in India to search for god, but at that moment, I felt more far away than ever.' I'm going to Delhi now and will catch the first plane home. What I saw of Hinduism totally disappointed me. They don't know who the founder is so there's no one to follow. They have only got self-appointed gurus and the only one I met, as far as I was concerned, was evil. And from what others have told me about the ones they met, many appeared to be all tarred by the same brush. I met several women who told me that when their husbands couldn't make them pregnant, they went to a temple and the priest did the job. One American woman of about 40 was several months pregnant and the priest told her that the child would be a son and be born white and would always have a special aura about him. She was to bring him back after five years for his blessing. But I'm always thinking about what my auntie told me about her faith in Jesus Christ and, as soon as possible, I'm going to see her and find out what I can about it. She's such a quiet peaceful person and I realise now that she has the answer.' I had a copy of the book of Luke with me, so I gave it her suggesting she read it first.

But my new friend insisted that there is no doubt that some of these holy men have been a great help to many people who were searching for the real meaning of life. Some give very good practical teaching of everyday life. The problem is their teaching does not bring a sense of being forgiven and cleansed of sin and given peace of heart and the assurance that we will spend eternity in heaven.

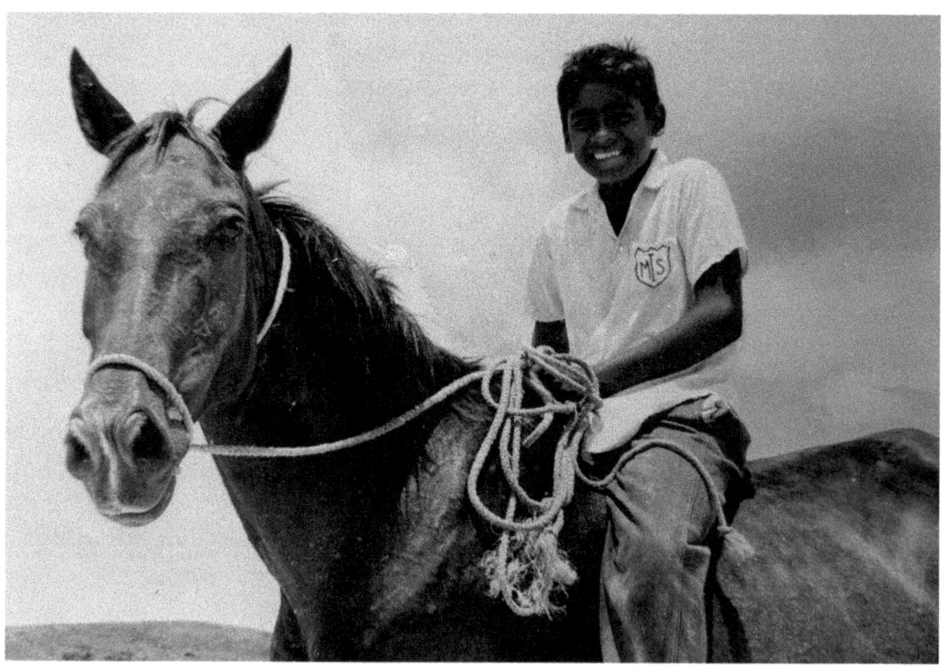

CHAPTER FIVE

CALCUTTA – KOLKATA

I was in Calcutta on one of the city's important anniversaries when there was a furious argument going on in the newspapers as to its true origin. There are several theories, and these include the name of a small village, a flat land, some land with no name, a canal, the ground of the goddess kali. There is even an unproven story that an Englishman asked a local the name of the place. He had been cutting the grass and not understanding the question, simply said 'kalcut' – the grass is cut. An Englishman, Job Charnock, landed there in 1690 and set up a trading post between three small villages. The issue was presented to the High Court in 2003 and it ruled Charnock was not the founder – there wasn't one. Incidentally this court was the first High Court in India being set up 1862.

Our office, known as Calcutta Bible House, is in a primary position in the city on Chowringhee Road. Built in 1811 and features a remarkable staircase made of Burmese teak. The staff were so proud of it and when the rest of the building became rather tired looking, they always polished the staircase every day. The British & Foreign Bible Society, founded in 1804, built a Bible House in nearly every capital of the world, usually in the centre of the capital city, and the Calcutta one was the second built after London. A shop on the ground floor was rented to an optician who operated from it for many years, paying only the original rent as the law prevented any change despite inflation. Nearby is Sudder Street with its several inexpensive hotels and good restaurants and a number of nefarious establishments.

I often stayed in a hotel near the office owned by a family known as Anglo Indians. But Rosie Smith, the owner when I was there, told me that she inherited it from her Armenian mother who managed the hotel till her death at 94 in 2014. Her grandparents were Armenian and had fled their country after the cruel Turkish invasion in 1915 and somehow landed up in Calcutta. They bought the hotel in 1936. The building is magnificent being built in 1783 and has lots of interesting features like the grand staircase to the first floor made of Burmese teak. There was no air conditioning but lots of ancient fans. Rosie insisted that she was proudly Anglo Indian because of her education and upbringing and chatted with me many times about her English heritage and how she loved to go to London every year. I hear that a member of the Oberoi family has now bought it and may possibly change its character.

When I checked *Trip Advisor* I saw that some guests likened it to a museum. That's true because of the vast array of historical photos and colonial style furniture like couches, chairs, tables, clocks and lamps.

> The hotel is located in the heart of the city only minutes' walk to the Indian Museum and a 6-minute stroll to the nearest underground metro station. It's also 2.3 km from the landmark Victoria Memorial and it's park . The rooms feature free Wi-Fi, flat-screen TVs, mini fridges, and tea and coffee making facilities. Complimentary perks include full English and Indian breakfast and parking. Other meals including, traditional afternoon tea and cakes, are offered in the Imperial dining room, as well as on a terrace balcony on the 1st Floor. There's also a relaxed guest lounge and a garden café.

If the Fairlawn was full, I stayed at the Lytton hotel nearby before it was refurbished. One time when I was on the second floor, right outside my window was the footpath where a family of five lived. I observed them over several days. They considered a five metre stretch of pavement as their place. One part was like the lounge and kitchen where they sat and cooked their meals and the other end was the sleeping area. Several times a day one of the children would sweep their area and around the fire hydrant nearby for this was their bathroom. These were not uneducated poorly clad beggars, but a family driven from their home in the countryside where constant drought had made it impossible to grow their food. The land owner had driven them off his land because they were no longer productive and able to pay their long-standing debts.

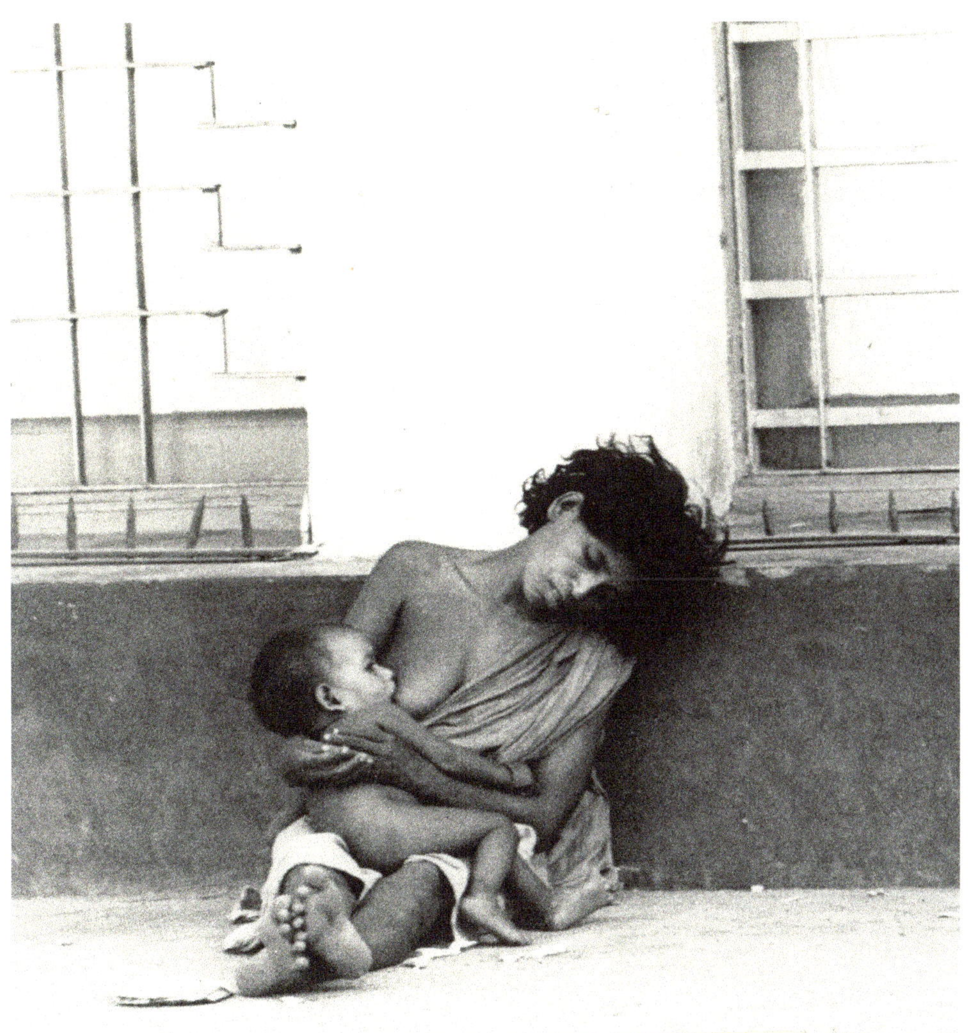

This is award-winning photo on the subject of Poverty. Said the judges, 'It depicts sadness and simplicity, solace and suffering.'

One evening after dinner I took a walk around the area. Within minutes a man approached me and asked if I'd like a tour guide. He was much older than me and wore a grey moustache. He pointed out the various small hotels and restaurants even describing the cuisine offered in each place. He cunningly described each establishment like the quality of the service, the food and even the class of prostitutes available there. 'An important part of this city is this area here,' he said waving his arms up a side street. Come I will show you.'

We entered what appeared to be a café but turned out to be a private brothel. There were a few standing about and after greeting them they were keen to chat. One young woman said, 'I'm trying to tell my friends not to go in there and then asked me about my job. When I mentioned Bible Society she said, 'Oh I've always wanted a Bible but I don't know how to get one.

I told her about my work and suggested she go to the Bible House and talk to the man at the front desk and ask him for a book that will help her find salvation. 'It's true we all need salvation from our sins,' she said. 'My parents spend a lot of money on it at our temple in Kathmandu. I'm from Nepal.' I explained the Good News of the Gospel to her and urged her to get the book.

On one of my many visits to India I was accompanied by Joy Aldred, an English writer (suitably chaperoned of course) who recorded this interview in Calcutta Bible House. This is the man I encouraged the prostitute to see.

> Mr Puling Behair Chatterjee was 45 years old when his life changed. As a Hindu Orthodox priest he had many disciples to teach, a large piece of land, and was the head of the most respected family in his town. In 1973 his life changed dramatically. This is how he described his experience.
>
> Our society hates Christianity, but at that particular time I felt something different in my heart. I followed our Hindu Scriptures, but they did not satisfy me. This worried me very much. So, with my wife, who also had no peace, I began a pilgrimage in search of truth. Then my son was found to have tuberculosis and the doctor said that he should go to hospital but my wife refused to send him because she believed her god would cure him. There was much crying and fasting as she pled with her gods in the temple, but no response. One day, I felt so depressed that I decided to end my life. I was crying to my god for help. I had been following the traditions and requirements of my faith but nothing happened. So I was very sorrowful in my mind.
>
> I travelled to Varanasi the most holy city of all for Hindus. I was walking by what we call the holy river Ganges, contemplating suicide when a lady noticed my agitated

state and boldly asked me where I was going. I told her that I was looking for god. She told me that I needed to meet the living God. The living god, did she know him, would she help me? She said she would and took me to a Christian church. I told her I that hated Christ and had never believed in him, but she told me that if I wanted to know the living God I should talk to the priest in the church and tell him what I was looking for.

I went to the priest and sat down in his office and he looked at me very carefully and said nothing. He could see that I was in a very sorrowful state of mind. He was silent for about five minutes and then gave me a glass of water and asked me why I had come. I explained that I was a Brahmin priest and I had come to ask about God.

He said: "All right, go back to your home and after three days, come here and eat with me and tell me how your son is." How did he know that my son was ill because I never told him? Then I felt a strange and wonderful peace in that room. As a Brahmin I could never eat food prepared by a Christian nor eat with one, yet in a strange way I felt in my heart that I should agree.

I went back to my house and did not tell my wife. After two days I saw that my son was better and I began to hope. A day later and he was beginning to improve. I was astonished. I had done so many things, even visiting the Muslim temple, and none was effective.

I went back to the priest and told him that my son was much better. He explained that it was the Lord Jesus Christ who had helped my son. That was the first time I had heard the full name 'the Lord Jesus Christ.' He gave me a New Testament and told me to read it and try to understand it. He asked me if I knew about the Bible – and I did not! He showed me how to find the Gospel of John.

Back at home I began to read John's gospel. Chapter 1 verse 1 spoke of a 'Word.' "In the beginning was the Word."

I was astounded because in Hinduism there is also a

Word – Brahma, which is the creator of the world. Only a priest's family can speak or use this word in any way and the Brahmin child uses it like a prayer. So here was this word, 'the creator.' I was wondering what was the New Testament meaning by the 'Word' – in Hinduism it signifies one supreme spirit.

I set about reading the Gospel of John very carefully. I began to understand it, more importantly I was beginning to understand myself through the words of John 1

v. 14– 16.

"The Word became a human being

and lived with us.

We saw His true glory,

the glory of the only Son of the Father

From Him all the kindness and all the truth of God

have come down to us.

John spoke of Him and shouted, "This is the one I told you would come! He is greater than I am, because He was alive before I was born.

Because of all that the Son is, we have been given one blessing after another."

I was beginning to see that I was in darkness. I kept on reading very carefully and soon found some more startling words in chapter three that touched me deeply.

"For God so loved the world that he gave his only son, that whoever believes in him will not perish but have everlasting life."

I understood that I was a sinner, before that I had never thought that I was a sinner because I was a priest. Priests are pure and holy; they even control the spiritual life of the people. I just knew that what I was reading was the truth.

So I started following the commandments of Jesus Christ in my daily life. I became a Christian. I told my wife about this Good News and she understood and prayed asking the true God to forgive her sins.

After I became a Christian I went to the villagers and told them about our conversion and that from now on we would live a Christian life and that I could no longer help them in their worship at the Hindu temple. There were more than fifty families who looked up to me as their priest. All this came as a dreadful shock to them. A few of my pupils began to despise and hate me. My nearest relatives hated me for what I had done and forced me to leave my house, but I believed God would provide for me.

My conversion was such a real experience for me that I wanted to spread God's Word to non-believers. I had the opportunity to begin working at the Bible Society in their large Bible House in downtown Kolkata. I was very happy. I improved my life and understanding of the Bible, and I felt very satisfied and peaceful. Sometimes though when problems come I read the Bible, and through this I realise my defects and correct my behaviour. Then my son became a Christian. He was completely healed within six months of going to meet the Christian pastor.

After 1980, my relative's attitudes began to change and even the village people would come to my house to discuss personal problems. They could see that the change in our lives had been so dramatic that perhaps we could help them too. My daughter also became a Christian.

Working at the Bible Society's bookshop, I meet people of all walks of life. I tell them: "Christianly is not a religion, it is the way of truth and life." Many Hindus come to the bookshop, wanting to find out about the Bible. I talk with them and ask them if they are sinners. They say they are not, but I tell them that they are sinners. We discuss and finally they agree with me. I tell them about the Bible and the Lord Jesus Christ. They come to understand, and I ask them if they want a Bible.

Some people say that the Bible is literature, some say it is philosophy, some people believe the Bible is history while others accept it has moral values. But they do not believe that Jesus is the saviour – just a great man. When I discuss it with them I ask if they are Hindu and they tell me they are. I tell them what my name is, and from that they know that I am a Brahmin. I tell them to read the passage in John chapter one and I ask them to think about it. Up to twenty five people will come here each day, mainly Hindus and Muslims. The Christians come but they run upstairs and ask for a discount because of the quantities they buy, so I mainly deal with the Hindus and Muslims and they respect me as a Brahmin. I tell them that Christianity isn't a religion, it is a reality – it is love. Every day I get up at 3.00 am do my exercises, bathe and from 5.00 to 6.00 am I have complete meditation, reading the Bible and finding out how to correct my defects.

Day by day my life improves as I understand more about the Bible. The Bible Society is the House of the Word – it is a very precious place because we are dealing with the Word of God and no other thing. The Bible Society is able to reach the un-reached people through the Bible. Please pray for us, it is a great responsibility. Thanks be to God, that through then Bible he talks to people and brings them light – so many are in darkness.

Perhaps I was being very stupid because many people consider this to be a very dangerous area of the city, but I was simply following the advice of the office manager when he said, 'Tonight take a walk around the area where you stay and see for yourself what Calcutta is like. You'll find all the extremes of life here.' It was true. One of the city's best hotels was close by, the Grand Hotel where I couldn't afford to buy my dinner. But on the pavement outside fancy boutiques were men selling delicious street food for a few cents. Street food is usually very good but its always wise to watch it being cooked.

One time when my usual hotels were full I stayed at an old one in central Calcutta that dated back to the British raj grandly named the Bengal Chambers. It appeared to be a couple of hundred years old. The lift was simply an open steel cage operated by an elderly gent who had spent his entire life manually driving guests up and down the four floors. 'I came into this lift job straight from school,' he said, 'and soon I will retire.'

'I was assigned a three-room suite along with a personal bearer or servant called *a khitmatgar.* He carried my luggage to the room and offered to unpack my suitcase and hang up the clothes. It was his job to take care of me, make the bed, clean the room, do the laundry and wait on me at the table. His caste prevented him from doing two other jobs, cleaning the toilet and my shoes. He said he would clean everything in the bathroom except the toilet. Another fellow came in every day for this. Yet another came for the shoes. He brought me the traditional 'bed tea,' – a cup of tea and biscuit brought to my room instead of a wakeup call. It was important not to lock the room door at night so that he had access in the morning. I would wake up to a voice saying, 'Here is your bed tea sir.'

The bedroom of the suite was as large as the lounge at home with a 20ft (6 metres) ceiling. There was a king-sized bed with a frame for a mosquito net. An ornate stand, which in itself was a valuable antique, held a large porcelain bowl and a jug of water the proper name of which was a 'pitcher set' and dated back to the Victorian era. These were valuable heirlooms. The date on the underside of the bowl was 1888. Under the bed was an old fashioned and beautifully decorated porcelain chamber pot. Another antique. Why a chamber pot when through the door was a modern toilet? Albeit one that seemed to follow Mr. Crapper's original design with a water tank attached high up the wall and a long chain. The bathroom was furnished with a traditional Victorian bath standing on four ornate legs, or would that be claw feet! It was perfectly clean but much of the enamel had worn off revealing its brass structure. The taps that miraculously produced hot and cold water were polished down to their copper piping. The hotel was built before electricity was available so all the wiring was attached to the outside of the walls. I shuddered to think of cleaners dusting these, as here and there, the copper wiring showed through. The daily fee was Rp200.

The approach to the hotel was a display of 'awful poverty, dirt, rubbish, pigs, dogs – one with half a leg missing, plus a dead one lying on the footpath.'

At the time when I was in charge of Compassion International's child sponsorship programme in India, I escorted the International Director and the Internal Auditor from the USA to various parts of the country, including Calcutta. I was determined to show them something of the colonial days so took them to stay at this Raj-style hotel. As we ascended to the reception on the first floor in the ancient elevator, my American colleagues expressed amazement at this steel cage that ground its way up. 'Surely we are not staying here.' After getting their keys they were introduced to their individual bearers. Their work was explained to them and I urged them to let him do their work and not try to disturb them by refusing their services. They couldn't believe the service like at dinner their bearer stood behind them. Every time someone took a mouthful of water, the bearer immediately refilled the glass. Next morning they said that their pyjamas were neatly set out on the bed that was turned down. They couldn't believe that a hotel of this vintage was still in operation. But that night, according to my tiny Sony short-wave radio, the stock market failed in New York and when I shared this news to them, it took their minds off their accommodation as they worried about the society's invested pension funds. My diary notes that the Americans 'couldn't believe we would stay there.'

But when speaking of hotels in this great city, one must mention the one 'fondly referred to as the Grand Dame of Chowringhee, The Oberoi Grand has been an icon on the landscape of Kolkata, the City of Joy for more than a century.' *Oberoi Hotels & Resorts*. But my budget wouldn't allow more than afternoon tea.

CHAPTER SIX

TRAMS AND RAILWAYS

Calcutta's first electric trams began running in 1902. By the look of some of them, they appear to be the originals that were first introduced in 1880 when they were horse-drawn. They are old and decrepit and rattle around the town, but they keep going. The official website describes the service in rather quaint English as follows:

> 'Tram lends Kolkata an old-world charm and add to the romantic element to the city. This slow moving, electrical reptile in narrow and crowded streets completes the ultimate attraction of the city. Having glided down the rails as a historian witness. Tram has itself been turned into an immemorial heritage for which the whole Kolkatans will be proud of.'

The first trams were hauled by horses imported from Kabul, Afghanistan. But many died due to the hot and humid weather conditions. Special hats were produced for the protection of the horses but after a few years the system was electrified.

Several people told me that they would never travel on the underground railway currently being built. As one rather unkindly said, 'Look at the way they run their trams, fancy that down below!' But to the credit of everyone concerned the first line was opened 24th October 24, 1984 covering a distance of 3.4 km. Ten years later there were 50 stations on the 59.38 kilometres (36.90 miles) metro.

But along with all other great cities of the world that built underground railways, the population suffered many years of traffic chaos and disruption. I do not recall how many people assured me that the metro was only a dream. Although I was an official correspondent of the *International Railway Journal* for Asia, I was not required to write about this venture as it was left to a local man. We sometimes discussed his problem of getting the real story, but I told him to ignore the politics and write only the facts.

INDIAN RAILWAYS IN CALCUTTA

On 15th August 1854, East Indian Railway's first train commenced its inaugural commercial run from Howrah to Hooghly (24 miles – 38km). There was just a single line and the original station was a simple one-roomed red brick building. This has grown into a magnificent structure. Today a total of 252 Mail/Express trains and 520 local passenger trains are handled from the 23 platforms of Howrah station daily carrying about 900,000 passengers.

Whenever I had the time I would go down to the station and observe not just the railway traffic but the huge numbers of people who have made their home there. They camp on the platforms, in alcoves, in the extensive basement areas – they are everywhere. There are hundreds of complete families plus an unknown number of street children. One social worker told me that she guessed there were about a thousand homeless children living in the station. Some of them earn a little money by doing odd jobs like one ten year old girl who told me she would go to the nearest market and steal fruit and bring it to sell to passengers. She was one of a family of six kids whose parents had abandoned them. A social worker told me about the tricks they get up to as they search for food. One family of five would select a group seated on a platform waiting for a train. They would have their luggage around them. The father would instruct the two eldest girls to do a sexy dance, and while the travellers were distracted, the rest of kids would try and steal their food. They would dart in, grab what they could, and race off up the platform and down the stairs to a basement. As soon as a young child could run it was included in the family's escapades.

With the help of a social worker, who translated the Bengali into English, I chatted with one family. First of all I gave the father a handsome tip and he was very happy to chat. His wife gave me a piece of cloth to sit on. They had a plot of land but had to give it up after several failed harvests. They had borrowed money for seed each year until they owed so much to the money lenders they had to quietly escape from the district and come to Calcutta. They crept out of the village one night and walked for many days, eating only once a day. They had five children but two died on the way, 'because they had nothing to eat,' said the father. The eldest girl with them sat close to me and quietly touched my leg and whispered, 'come with me,' as she put her arm around me and said something in Bengali.

She was only about ten. Her mother saw her and secretly waved her fingers to me that seemed to suggest it was ok to go with her. How sad to think that this young kid would soon descend into prostitution but that's what poverty and hunger will do. Starving parents and siblings would cause this.

'Do you know what that young girl said to you?' asked my guide. 'She said, I'm getting breasts and you can have them.'

One day while standing on a platform observing a train, three small boys in dirty ragged clothing, aged about eight or nine, came along and, right there in front of me, one collapsed and died. I looked at a man standing nearby and asked 'What can we do about it?' He just shrugged his shoulders and said, 'He was probably hungry,' and walked away. The two companions stared at him for a few moments and scurried away.

An essay by Adrian Levy & Cathy Scott-Clark entitled The Wrong Side of the Tracks and found in Simon Winchester's *Calcutta* is a fascinating description of Howrah station and especially of the numerous children to be found there. Written in November 2002 they write: "It seems an incredible story, to lose a child in the crush of a railway station for years, or for ever, but everything about Indian railways is larger than life: 37,000 miles of track, 7,000 train running daily, serving more than 3.7 billion passengers yearly, the world's largest employer, retaining more than 1.6 million staff. Every one of its major termini is a disorienting world for a new comer. They describe the condition of the numerous children there as "drowning in a deluge of Ds: deficiency, disease, disability, destitution, dropping out of school, delinquency, diffidence, drugs, din, dust and dirt.' Nobody cares if they live or die."

Calcutta gives the impression of being a decaying city of open sewers and overflowing garbage, of millions of slum dwellers and an estimated 400,000 homeless people who must struggle daily for survival. The city overflows with migrants from the countryside and refugees from the recurring disasters in Bangladesh. The population doubled in 30 years to 11 million, outpacing the government's ability to house or educate its citizens. A recent survey estimated that Calcutta has 56,000 homeless children under 18, more than half of them between 6 and 10. One in three do some work. Some sell goods they have stolen and others work in shops or garages. About 8% are household helpers; 9.3% are classified as beggars.

But this great city is home to numbers of educated and prosperous people. Calcattans are very proud of their city. It was here that the cause of malaria was discovered in 1902, by surgeon-major Ronald Ross for which he was awarded the Nobel Prize. Most notable was the writer Rabindanathn Tagore. I love these few lines from one of his poems:

Another creature apart from me lives in my room
For the same rent:
A lizard.
There's a difference between him and me:
He doesn't go hungry.

At dusk I go to the Sealah station.
Spend the evening there
To save the cost of light.
Engines chuffing.
Whistles shrieking.
Passengers scurrying.
Coolies shouting.
I stay till half past ten.
Then back to my dark, silent, lonely room.

Calcutta was established in the year 1686 when the British were expanding their role in India. On 24 August, 1690 one of the businessmen of the British India Company, Joe Charnock, selected a site between villages on the Hooghly River and pitched his tent there and began trading. Very quickly a community grew around him. The growth continued apace until it became the second largest city in India. But at the time when there was much unrest, the British had to send in a force to establish control. Their controversial leader, General Clive described it in 1798 as 'one of the most wicked places in the universe, rapacious and luxurious beyond conception.' He did not have the local people in mind when he said that.

The population during the 1980's was ten million or more than twice the number of my own country of New Zealand. At the time of writing, it had risen to about eighteen million. 'But it might be much more than that,' said a City Council official, waving his arm around the crowded street, 'I don't think a lot of these were counted.'

But there is no place on earth that is so complicated, varied in every way, almost indescribable, a 'city of almost unimaginable extremes, splendid and horrifying, exhilarating and shaming,' wrote Paul Theroux. This city attracted many rich traders who built substantial family homes, some recognised as palaces. Soon it became known as the city of palaces. But with the number of people flooding in from the rural areas where drought had ruined their livelihood, there was a great shortage of houses. Settlements of people called *bastis*, where about one-third of the city's population lives. The majority of *basti* dwellings are tiny, unventilated, single-story rooms. They have few sanitary facilities, and there is very little open space.

I found a photography shop and met the son of the owner whom I discovered later was a well-known cricket photographer, Srenik Sett. We became good friends. He offered to introduce me to two famous people, Mother Teresa and the scion of the city's main land owners. At that time the catholic nun was not so well known and I passed on that. To this day I regret that decision. Many years later we did meet at an airport in South India I was able to give her a copy of the newly published *Good News Bible*.

Srenik was anxious to buy my Hasselblad camera, which was quite rare in India. I promised him that on my next visit I would bring him one. I regularly carried about 9 kg of equipment but this camera, too heavy to carry in my camera bag, could be divided up into four sections, so I packed them in my luggage. The part that held the film looked like a metal box. When the customs officer found it, he picked it up and asked, 'What is this?' He had just been examining my watch. At that moment, my watch beeped the hour and he nearly dropped the Hasselblad part. This was the time when digital watches that signalled the hour with a beep were all the rage in Hong Kong where I lived. They weren't available in India. He didn't wait for my answer but dropped it back into the suitcase and waved me on. I had a permanent request from friends to bring in small transistor radios – mostly to listen to the cricket.

CHAPTER SEVEN

THE MARBLE PALACE AND MARIGOLDS

My friend Srenik Sett knew the scion of the main landowners of the city and took me to visit him. He was a direct descendent of Raja Rajendra Mullick. He was a keen amateur photographer and he had asked to meet me in the hope I would help him build a darkroom. 'My house,' as he put it, is known as 'the Marble Palace,' built in 1835 and is famous for its marble walls, floors and sculptures. At that time it was still a private home and permitted no visitors so I was greatly honoured to be invited. It was home to the extended family and staffed by about 150 servants. Years later it became a major tourist attraction.

I was amazed at their collection of Western sculptures, Victorian furniture, and paintings by European and Indian artists. I'm no art connoisseur but I could see that they had some very fine paintings. There were countless chandeliers including one in the bathroom I used that was big enough for our lounge. Several were the largest I have ever seen. They are all lit by electricity but my host said that originally, they were lit by hundreds of candles. 'Imagine servants painstakingly lighting all those candles every night. They would have to start at the top else they would burn their arms!' There were numerous clocks of every kind including several majestic grandfather clocks. Everywhere there were huge Belgian floor to ceiling mirrors and many copies of Greek sculptures. Some of these were all jammed together on shelves and tables.

A large cupboard had been converted into a darkroom and the first thing I had to do was explain that a darkroom had to be absolutely dark. Not even the tiniest slither of light was allowed. I suggested he call a servant in to clean the enlarger as it was covered in dust, explaining that dust was the greatest enemy in a dark room. One tiny speck on a film will become a large blot on the print.

In addition to the 150 indoor servants (he wasn't sure of the exact number) there were another a team of about 50 gardeners, watchmen and zoo keepers. The private zoo was considered the first one in the country, although there some in other Maharaja palaces. The aviary had a variety of peacocks, toucans, storks, and cranes plus several chimpanzees, a giraffe, several rare white tigers and a couple of elephants.

There is an opening in a wall through which a large crowd of street dwellers is fed once a day. 'This is our Hindu custom,' explained our host. 'We give them a good serving of vegetarian food which is enough to sustain them for a day.' I was tempted to ask him how many times a day did he eat!

In later years this palace became an important tourist attraction. There was a time that Calcutta was known as the city of palaces because so many prominent businessmen moved here, building themselves ornate homes.

Many cities have an outstanding feature by which they are known, such as the Sydney Harbour bridge, the London bridge or the Golden Gate. Calcutta has one too – the Howrah bridge. This crosses the Hooghly River and is the main link between the two halves of Calcutta. Some travellers have described it as an ugly monstrosity but to Kalkutans it's a thing of beauty. It carries every day 100,000 vehicles comprising trams, buses, bullock carts and trucks. And 150,000 pedestrians, plus motorcycles and rickshaws easily making it the busiest cantilever bridge in the world. Its as though all of India is crossing the bridge and so its great fun to go to one end and watch all the people. It was third-longest cantilever bridge at the time of its construction. Its now the sixth-longest bridge of its type in the world with a central span of 1,600 ft (460m). In total it is 705m-long and 30m-wide bridge and was built in 1943.

MARIGOLDS

I had heard about the flower market on the banks of the Hooghly River, the Mullik Ghat, and was advised to go up onto the bridge and look down on what is a sea of colour. I got to know these flowers very well as they are the predominate blossoms in a welcome garland. Everywhere I went in India visiting schools and orphanages and poor communities we were supporting, I was garlanded with these flowers. Sometimes there were five or six placed around my neck but I have to confess I did not like their scent.

The flower market was an astonishing display of gold, red, orange and yellow that radiated up from beside the brown dirty river. There were hundreds of men buying and selling, shouting their prices. The ground around them was strewn with petals. Men and women were bringing in thousands of blossoms already made up into garlands, their carts, rickshaws, bicycles, and some, their heads, overladen with these colourful things. I was glad to learn that once garlanded with these smelly leis of flower, one could immediately take it off, and set them aside. Its the principle of being welcomed in this way that was the important thing, not so much as to decorate the visitor.

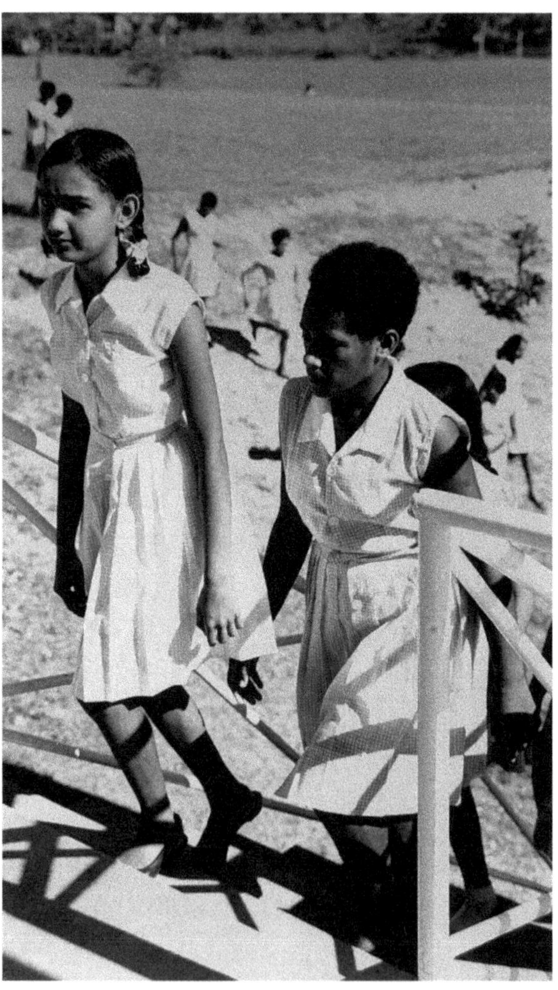

CHAPTER EIGHT

TEA MARKET

When I mentioned to a staff member that I wanted to buy some genuine Indian tea, he immediately sprang off his chair and said follow me. The tea market was just a short walk from the office. As we made our way along the crowded footpath he said, 'I am very proud that our consultant wishes to purchase the proper Indian tea and take it home to his loved ones. They deserve the best and I will show it to you.' It was a huge warehouse was lined with hundreds of tea chests. The tea was everywhere. It was scattered on the floor and floated in the air.

'Looks like you don't just drink tea here but simply breathe it in.' My host looked at me sideways not understanding.

"What kind of tea you like? Everything is here. Do you want strong, weak, black, green, from Darjeeling or Simla or anywhere?' A merchant was quick to seize the chance of a sale and recommend a blend of Darjeeling and Assam. He dug it out of two open sacks weighing it in an antiquated brass scale, and adding a little extra said, 'Your beloved will soon be asking you to come back and buy some more.' I asked him about his ancient scales. They were made of brass, and he said they were his grandfather's who weighed out many a bushel on them. His family had worked in this market for three generations. On our return to the office my friend called out, 'He has bought tea. He's bought tea.' The smiles all-around said I was a suitable guest to their great city.

As an interesting aside, it was the British who began cultivating tea in India and it wasn't long before it became the national drink. Tea is everywhere. The first time I bought tea at a railway station; it was served in a tiny clay cup. I asked, 'What do I do with this?'

'Oh, just throw it away.'

The tiny clay cup was not much bigger than an egg cup and the drink and cup cost only a couple of cents. Made of pure clay it was truly biodegradable. I soon learned to enjoy Indian tea. The water, tea leaves, sugar, milk and sometimes spices such as cardamon, ginger or cinnamon are all boiled up together. Tea is sold everywhere, on railway platforms, outside churches, hospitals and on every footpath. The English are known for their love for and dependence on tea, but the same could be said of India. Like one rickshaw driver in New Delhi said to me, 'two things we love, cricket and tea.'

This is how one major tea merchant describes their company's product:

> "The odyssey of the original Tosh's Tea dates back to 1916. An Indian tea brand, with its roots in the Pre-Independence Era, Tosh's Tea has pioneered blended and flavoured teas in the Indian domestic market. Our virtuosity in the art of blending tea has been an extraordinary phenomenon, enticing epicureans of different epochs."

Some tea vendors make a show of cooling the boiling tea by holding a can of tea at arm's length above the head and pouring it into another can or a cup held at the waist without spilling a drop.

I'm indebted to Victoria Fernandez © Culture Trip for the following description of this ancient drink:

> Though every country has its own word for tea, almost all pronunciations stem from just two root words: '*te*' and '*cha*.' Here is the story behind the world's words for tea.
>
> In the early years of tea cultivation in China, the leaves were unprocessed and had a bitter taste, earning the resulting drink the name '荼 tu', meaning 'bitter vegetable'. Mandarin's current word for tea, '茶 cha', didn't come into recorded existence until 760 C.E., when a scholar named Lu Yu wrote the *Cha Jing*, or the *Classic of Tea*, in which he mistakenly omitted a cross stroke from the character 'tu', resulting in a much different word: cha. (Look closely at these characters and notice the second one has a missing line.)
>
> For nearly a thousand years, tea stayed the secret of the East. Then, in the 1500s, the Portuguese arrived in China. They'd travelled to the Far East hoping to gain a monopoly on the spice trade. But soon after tasting the brew for the first time, the explorers quickly realised its potential and decided to focus on exporting tea instead.

The Portuguese called the drink cha, just like the people of southern China did. From the port of Canton – around modern-day Guangzhou – Hong Kong, and Macau, the Portuguese shipped the now-processed leaves down through Indonesia, under the southern tip of Africa, and back up to western Europe.

Around a 100 years after the Portuguese first discovered tea, the Dutch started shipping the leaf from China using their own trade routes. The Dutch first encountered tea in 1607 around the modern-day Fujian province, where Hokkien was the major language. Though the written character for tea was '茶', its pronunciation varied depending on the dialect. In Mandarin and Cantonese, for example, it's pronounced *'cha'*, whereas in Wu Chinese it's *'dzo'*. Following in the linguistic footsteps of the Hoklo folk of Fujian, the Dutch called the drink 'thee.'

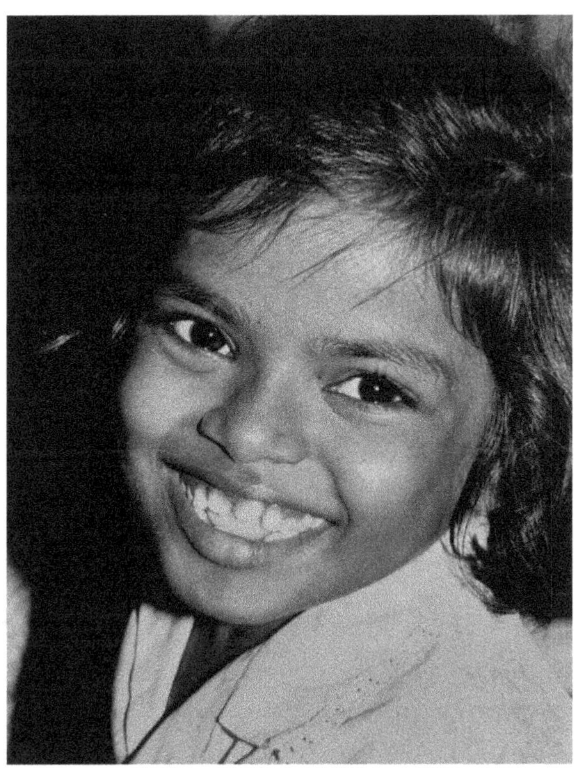

Marathi girl.

CHAPTER NINE

CALCUTTA SCHOOL

During the time when I was Director of Compassion International several Christian ladies in Calcutta asked if we could support them in starting a school for street children. They had already found a sponsor who could provide a large room in one of his houses in the central city. They needed money to provide school uniforms, a daily meal as well as simple school materials. Simple in the form of exercise books, pencils, a black board and chalk. All the children lived on the street as homeless orphans or with families. The women canvassed the streets for likely pupils and within a day had 100 kids keen to learn. They all turned up at 'the school' clad in their usual grubby clothes. A tailor who had a shop next door was able to run up simple dresses for the girls and shorts and shirts for the boys. He and his staff did this in 48 hours.

We decided that the first thing to do on arrival at school was to send them out onto the street and have a bath at the nearest fire hydrant. There were two close by. When a teacher told the girls to use one hydrant and the boys the other. One of the girls said, 'It doesn't matter, we know what they look like!' They ranged from about 6 to 12 years. They stripped off their clothes and danced around the hydrants splashing each other, so excited at the prospect of being in a school. They came back into the classroom naked and dripping wet and were given set of new clothes – the school uniform of blue dresses for the girls and blue shorts and white shirts for the boys. When classes were over, they were told to change back into their normal clothes, hanging their uniforms on nails along one wall. If they took them home, they would never be seen again as their parents were likely to sell them. So that was the daily procedure: first a bath, hang up their street clothes, change into school uniform. Then a good breakfast like *radha ballabhi*, a lentil stuffed Indian flat bread which is deep-fried in mustard oil served a spicy potato curry. After class, change back into street clothes and hang up their uniforms.

It was fascinating to observe how the teachers taught in two languages. First Bengali, like counting 1 to 10 then in English. 'They will need English in modern India,' said the head mistress. The kids were so keen to learn. None of them had ever sat still for more than a few minutes so it was remarkable how quickly they learned to concentrate on their lessons. To begin, the teachers decided that two hours was long enough and over time extended it to four hours.

Twelve months later the school was still going. Remarkably only ten kids had dropped out and the others were doing well. They had no desks but sat on the floor. As soon as I came into the room, they scrambled to their feet and chorused, 'Gud morning sah.' When they were told I was their sponsor they grinned from ear to ear and clapped. One girl stood up and said, 'We are divided into two groups called the 'The Taxi Wallahs,' and the 'The Rickshaw Wallahs,' i.e., the fast learners and the slow learners.

Many families and organisations ran small schools like this all over the city and from time-to-time government officials tried to close them down and incorporate them into government schools. 'But our kids will have none of it,' said our head mistress. 'They will never leave here. They know that we love them.'

Here are the notes of an address I gave to at the St Andrews Church in Hong Kong in 1975.

Last week I was in India. I was visiting children in our sponsorship programme. We have 15,098 sponsored children there. They are all from very poor homes. Many are orphans or the children of poor widows. Some are from families that are extremely poor whose parents are unable to adequately care for them. They find it difficult if not impossible to find the school fees and generally able to take good care of their children. I was asked to speak at a school assembly. About a thousand small children sat cross-legged on the floor and listened with rapt attention. For twenty minutes they sat without fidgeting or talking and gave me their undivided attention. I caught a plane home that day and a few minutes after landing, I was due to speak to a small group of boys at out church club. They would not sit quietly but wanted to chat and generally misbehave. What a contrast!

CHAPTER TEN

MOTHER TERESA AND WILLIAM CARY

Saint Teresa of Calcutta was almost unknown when I was first in Calcutta. When my new friend Srenik Sett offered to introduce me I declined, not knowing anything about her at the time – my greatest faux pas. Although many years later, Russell Self and I were both on the same flight as her out of Trivandrum and Russell grabbed my copy of the newly published Good News Bible and presented it to her. This modern day saint has done much to put Calcutta on the map. Although she is deeply revered around the world, even a Noble Prize recipient, there are many citizens of the city who believe she has done them much harm. They dislike the way her work among the poorest of the poor and the destitute, has given them all such a bad name. As one fellow said to me. 'That a foreign woman should deign to criticise my great city…' He went on, 'Everybody thinks we are like that, leaving people to live in great poverty having no care for them.'

'What do you do for the poor in your neighbourhood,' I asked him.

'There's no one like that where I live. We are all educated Bengalis with a proud history. If there are any poor, they probably come from Bihar.'

'Don't you feel a responsibility to help them?

'No of course not, as I said, they come from Bihar.'

WILLIAM CARY

I was ten years old when I was given a present from my Sunday School teacher at Lahore Street Hall, Wairoa – *William Carey, The Pioneer Missionary to India's Millions.* I still have it in my library. I remember being fascinated by the fact that at the same age as me, when I was struggling to learn my own mother tongue, William learned by heart nearly the whole of Dyche's Latin vocabulary. Born in 1761, by the time he was in his teens he had a profound knowledge of birds, insects and plants. In later years he became Asia's best informed scholar of these subjects. As a kid after one lesson in Greek, he was so fascinated he taught himself Greek. He then self-taught himself Hebrew, Dutch, German and French. He married at twenty but his wife suffered from mental distress and at times became quite ill. But Carey distinguished himself by the way he cared for her.

Carey lived in Calcutta when he first arrived in India but after finding the cost of living there too high, and the opposition of the East India Company, moved to the village of Hooghly then to a Danish settlement at Serampore a few miles further south.

This is a summary by *Wikipedia*: 'William Carey (17 August 1761 – 9 June 1834) was an English Christian missionary, translator, social reformer and cultural anthropologist who founded the Serampore College and the Serampore University, the first degree-awarding university in India.

'He went to Calcutta (Kolkata) in 1793, One of his first contributions was to start schools for impoverished children where they were taught reading, writing, accounting and Christianity. He opened the first theological university in Serampore offering divinity degrees, and campaigned to end the Hindu practice of sati.

'The Asiatic Society commended Carey for "his eminent services in opening the stores of Indian literature to the knowledge of Europe and for his extensive acquaintance with the science, the natural history and botany of this country and his useful contributions, in every branch."

'He translated the Hindu classic, the *Ramayana*, into English, and the Bible into Bengali, Oriya, Assamese, Marathi, Hindi and Sanskrit. He also produced dictionaries of six languages. Incredibly, he guided the translation of the New Testament and / or the Bible in twenty six languages and dialects. The quality of his Bengali translation of the Bible has never been equalled. William Carey has been called a reformer and illustrious Christian missionary.'

VARANASI

Varanasi is one of the world's oldest continuously inhabited cities – and the holiest for Hindus' Varanasi, may be India's spiritual capital.

"Almost every Hindu household in Varanasi has an altar dedicated to Shiva in the house. Eating meat at home is unthinkable," explained Abhishek Shukla, a *shastri* (priest) at Varanasi's famous Kashi Vishwanath temple. "Staying sattvic is a priority for those who wish to attain salvation because we believe that our souls would suffer like those we killed for food otherwise. Meat, onions and garlic exacerbate *tamasic* (the opposite of sattvic) tendencies, making it difficult for people to concentrate and exercise good judgement."

Traditionally, many Varanasi restaurants have served meat to cater to Western tourists and non-vegetarian Hindu pilgrims, and local sattvic cuisine was primarily eaten at home. But in 2019, the Hindu-nationalist BJP government banned the sale and consumption of meat within a 250m radius of all Varanasi temples and heritage sites.

The 2019 meat ban has fostered creativity among a new generation of chefs in Varanasi. There is a growing number of restaurants serving local sattvic or plant-based recipes. Today, locals estimate are anywhere from 40 to 200 sattvic restaurants in Varanasi, a huge jump since the 2019 meat ban.

The sight of baked or dried cow dung cakes is something that it takes visitors a bit of getting used to. In fact, as diners enter, they are greeted by the sight of dried cow dung cakes stacked up to the ceiling in an outdoor shed. A genuine restaurant does everything in-house, from pounding their spices in stone mills to grinding the flour for the baati. The vegetables for the accompanying chokha made with eggplant, potatoes and tomatoes, are also roasted on top of the same dung cakes, before simmering in a spice mix in clay pots.

One guide said that many tourists have told him that the food in Varanasi is the best food they have ever eaten in India." Millions of visitors come to Varanasi every year.

I spoke to an elderly Hindu priest on the river bank. He wore a faded yellow gown and had four thick white strips across his forehead. He told me he had been a priest all his life and had remained a bachelor so he could 'worship the gods without interruption.'

'I suppose you have been seeking salvation from sin all your life?'

'Yes, I have.'

'Have you found it yet?'

'No, of course not.'
'Why not. You have many gods.'
''Yes, true, but they don't give salvation. I just have to keep on worshipping and hope for a better life next time.'

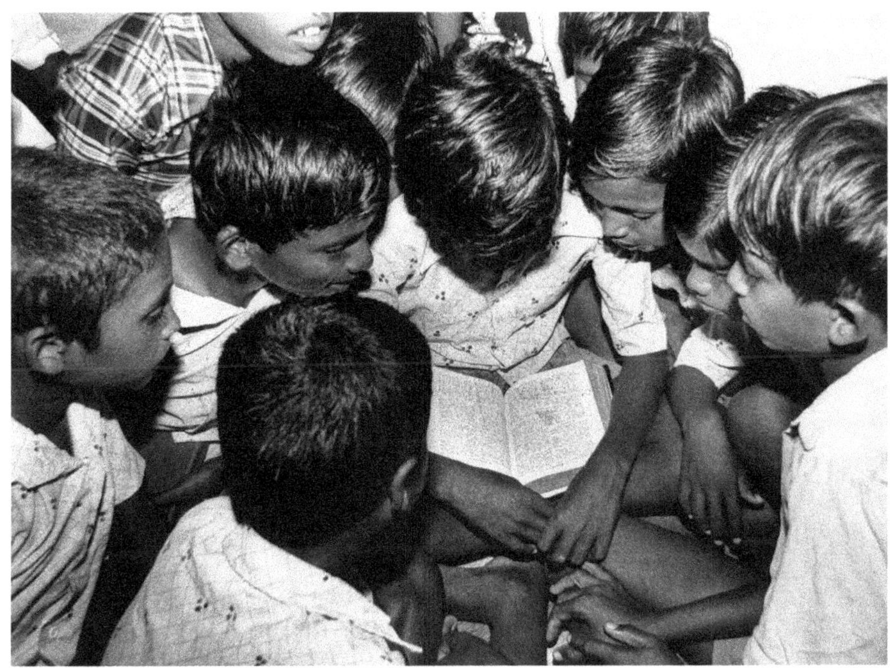

Tamil boys.

CHAPTER ELEVEN

SERVANTS

One time when a flight was cancelled late at night, I was put into a nearby one-star hotel. I got to bed at about midnight but after a few minutes there was a knock on the door. I opened it and a man pushed past me and began to sweep out the room with a straw broom. I let him be and when he had finished, stood by the door moving his hand up and down signifying he expected a tip. I had been back in bed for just a few minutes when there was another knock. This time it was the bathroom wallah. He was of the caste that cleaned bathrooms and toilets. Back in bed after tipping him so that he would go away, another knock. It was room service who announced that the airline would like to offer me some refreshments. 'Just bring me some water.'

'Oh no sahib, no water, you will find it in the tap. Its only the coffee or tea available. He stood there waiting. 'I deserve my tip now thank you sahib.'

Back in bed I wondered if it were possible that there would be no more disturbances. But ten minutes later, another gentle tapping. 'I'm from reception sir enquiring if you want the wakeup call at 5 am? The plane goes at six." The rascal could have used the phone but delivered the message personally in hope of a tip. Unbelievingly a few minutes later there was another knock from the reception. 'Sorry sir, I was mistaken, you must check in at five so I had better call you at four.' It was now two am.

I had a few bad nights in hotels like one in Ranchi called The Fertiliser Plant Trainees Hotel – Bed bugs and mosquitoes kept me awake until 4.30 am. Later I discovered that if there were bed bugs it was best to wear clothing that covered all of the body as the bugs are only looking for bare skin. The other was to avoid them is to carry a large plastic sheet.

I always stayed in old raj-era hotels where I could. Visiting the twin cities of Hydrabad-Secunderabad gave me the opportunity of staying in the old Percy's Hotel that dates back to the turn of the century. An ancient well-used menu card was presented at each meal. Dinner the first night I was there was: Chicken soup, Fried fish & chips and salad, Mutton puliso, Chicken curry, Fruit trifle.

Secunderabad was an interesting city. It has an amazing collection of churches some dating back several centuries. The church of our lady of Sorrows dates back to the 16th and 17th centuries where the Nizam, King of Deccan had his palace. There is a story how this church came into existence. A devoted French missionary priest lived in a cave on Jahanuma hill, spending time in prayer, penance and fasting and performing miracles. During a severe drought, the Nizam called him and asked him to pray for rain. He agreed on the condition that the Nizam would provide land to build the church of our Lady of Sorrows. The Nizam agreed. The priest fasted and prayed and there was heavy rain. The Nizam kept his word and gave them land where the first church in that part of the country was built. When the Nizam died in 1937, he was considered the richest man in the world. He had a collection of 350kg of diamonds and uncountable gold pieces.

Here is an interesting piece about servants:

Servants: A Downstairs History of Britain from the Nineteenth Century to Modern Times, by Lucy Lethbridge, Norton, 2013), Kindle Loc. 1718-1740:

> The servant in India conducted his work with a commitment that even in Britain would have been hard to command. The duties, for example, of the *khitmatgar,* or bearer, might include standing behind his master's chair at mealtimes and stirring his tea, cutting his meat – everything short of actually eating the food for him. By the mid-1920s, even the most self-important pukka sahib found this kind of behaviour a little embarrassing.
>
> Her servants were generally the first people from whom the Raj housewife, if she were curious, learned about India. There were the minutely calibrated differences in religious observance and caste to begin with. Intricate sectarian distinctions meant that each job came with its own religious significance to be carefully respected. The cook (always a man) would not touch pork if he were a Muslim or beef if he were a Hindu.

The *khitmagar,* who had the task of managing the other servants, would not undertake anything but his own tasks; even moving an article of furniture would be beneath him. The work of sweeping, scrubbing or emptying chamber pots was done only by Untouchables; the work of looking after dogs by yet another caste – and often a young child. Untouchables would not handle dead animals, the disposal of which required the services of another group altogether, and the Goddens remembered that 'if a crow fell dead into our garden or one of our guinea-pigs died, Nitai, our sweeper could not pick up or touch the corpse; a boy of a special sect had to be called in from the bazaar; he put on his best shirt of marigold-coloured silk to do this grisly work'.

Most servants were men, with the exception of the *ayah,* who was the household nanny, but the cook *khan sama* would often have helping him in the kitchen a *tunny-ketch,* a woman permitted to feed the poultry, grind the spices and cook the rice, attend to the lamps and clean the master's boots, work considered beneath the dignity of the cook.

A *musalchi* helped with the washing-up, a kind of scullion, described in 1890 by Flora Annie Steel: 'bearing, as his badge of office, a greasy swab of rag tied to a bit of bamboo'. In most large households, *derzi,* or tailor, endlessly stitching at clothes he was mending or copying, might be found sitting on the veranda; then there was the *dhobi,* who had the never-ending labour of the family's laundry (and most people changed at least twice a day in the heat, and then for dinner). In those places where there were no telephones, *chuprassis* were employed to send messages and acted as informal bodyguards, always on the lookout for people going in and out. And because many rural areas had no electricity and therefore no electric fans, there was also the *punkah-wallah* whose sole duty was to pull the rope that operated the fan, or *punkah,* day and night to create a cooling breeze. The night *punkah-wallah* could do it by fixing a rope to a foot and could perform the movement while almost asleep.

Most European women had no other contacts with the Indian people except with their servants, and perhaps, dignitaries met through their husband's work.

In 1894 Fanny Parkes wrote; To a person fresh from England, the number of servants attending a table is remarkable. We had only a small party of eight to dinner yesterday, including ourselves; three and twenty servants were in attendance! Each gentleman takes his own servants, in number from one to six, and lady her attendant or attendants, as it pleases her fancy.

I used to think that these were people from England who normally had servants at home but on reaching India multiplied them extranvently. Then I discovered that this fitted in quite well with the practice in India among the nobility and rich. Like the first time I travelled first class on a train. Our coach was divided into four-seat compartments. In some were a couple seated comfortably and outside in the corridor slept their servant lying across the door.

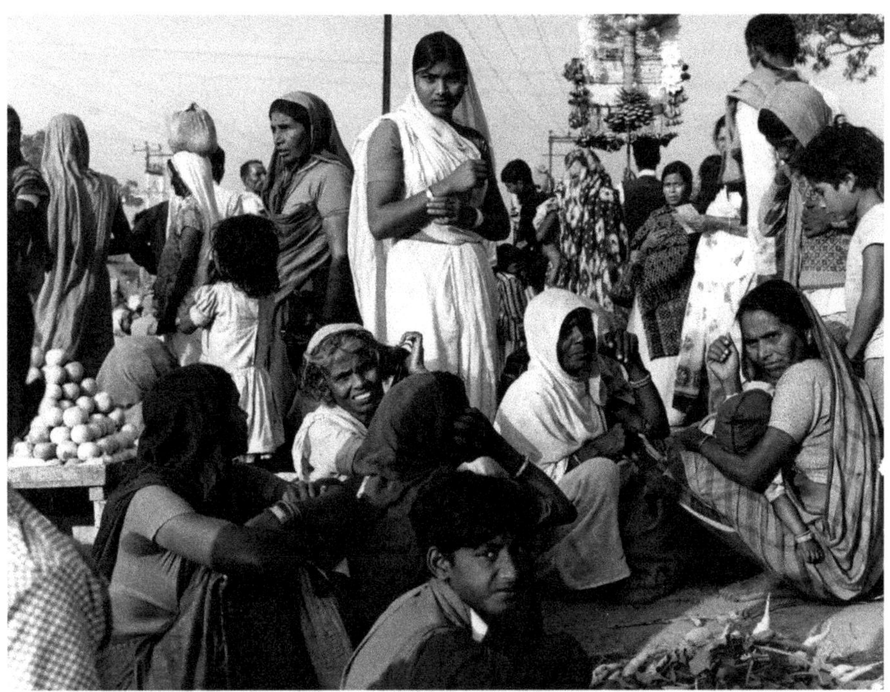

Women in rural market, Bihar.

CHAPTER TWELVE

MADRAS – CHENNAI

In my hotel in Madras was a painting of European woman being helped ashore on a sailing ship's lifeboat. She was being carried ashore the last few metres by a burly coolie and dumped in the sandy shore of what became one of India's largest cities created by foreigners. The Portuguese explorers were the first to settle here in 1504. Then came the Dutch, the French and lastly the English in 1693. Their trading attracted great number of local people and thus developed into an important city.

For Christians this is a place of significance because it is believed St Thomas, the disciple of Christ died here. According to Syrian Christian tradition, Thomas was killed with a spear at St. Thomas Mount in Chennai on 3 July in AD 72. His remains are said to reside in San Thomas Cathedral, first built in 1504. Down the road is St Mary's Church, the first English church built in India. He was purportedly killed on a hill in the city now called St Thomas Mount. When Zacharia, the Bible Society Secretary in Tamil Nadu asked me to help him with his driving lessons, we drove up this mountain. But I cautioned him saying that I didn't want to join St Thomas yet!

There is something different about Madras. It has its share of slums and beggars, but many of the original homesteads of the early settlers remain along with very old businesses like Spensers dating back to 1895 and became a great departmental store, and later a mall, the first in India. The city is more orderly than most others.

My favourite hotel in Madras, now Chennai, was the Connemara. It has now become one of the prestigious Taj group. Prior to its refurbishment by the Taj company into a top class establishment, it was a modestly priced and of good quality.

As their website puts it: If the Taj Connemara, Chennai could speak, it would tell you tales from its history, the place became a household name across the globe, for it was here where the blue-blooded indulged and entertained. But little did anyone know how history would shape the fate of the entire colonial empire, and this small but significant beginning of it. As the presidency of Madras became the metropolitan of Chennai, the iconic Connemara was entrusted into the hands of the Taj Management in 1984. Today, this symbolic 5 star hotel in Chennai has been carefully restored to its premier status with influences inspired by the past and present.

Somewhere I found this description "Enter the grand lobby through a foyer flanked by sepia-toned memories of a regal past. The refurbished grand wooden staircase embellished with South Indian stonework pays homage to the rich design culture of Chennai. Right across this, standing tall amidst the muted tones is the centuries-old brass statue of Shiva & Parvati amidst an aura of glittering deepams. The original lattice ceiling complements the Carrera marbled floor which paves the way to the personalised reception desks for a quick, efficient check-in. Business travellers will find themselves conveniently close to most of the city's business districts, while leisure travellers will find exhilaration in the city's cultural offerings. The Taj Connemara, Chennai has many stories to enthral you with, and you may be inspired to create a tamer version of your very own, here."

Wikipedia describes it as follows:

> The official version remains that the hotel was named "Connemara" in 1891 as a mark of respect for Robert Bourke, Baron of Connemara—a cultural district in Western Ireland—and then Governor of Madras. While in his official capacity he did a great deal for the development of Madras, he also had his share of flaws and very dangerous ones at that. He was an incurable womaniser and was generously offered Indian women from the harems of ruling nawabs. He also reportedly had intimate relations with his wife's own sister and the chambermaid.

Lady Connemara is supposed to have contracted STD from her husband. One day, she caught him red-handed with a group of young women and stomped out of the government house with her bags. Not sure where to go, she landed at the Connemara Hotel which was then called the Albany in 1890. She stayed there for about three months before she set sail for Ireland and promptly divorced her husband. It was a big case and Lord Connemara paid the price by losing his governorship of Madras. Many say that the hotel was actually named Connemara in 1891 to honour the troubled wife of the notorious baron.

The hotel houses a very good bookshop, probably the best one I ever found in India. The gift shop carried a range of finely made leather goods.

When I was a student in Auckland I had a Saturday morning job doing the garden at the hostel of the Christian Alliance of Women and Girls. Actually I hated gardening but there were always couple of nice girls to talk to and some of my fellow students were a bit jealous that I could do that. We weren't supposed to fraternise with the girls in our class. One day, one of them asked me to help her with a project about the railways she was doing for her teacher training course, which I was glad to do. Twenty years later we met up in Madras where she was working as a missionary. This was Colleen Redit. The title of her subsequent autobiography says it all, *Realising a Vision through Faith.*[7] I had been on Colleen's mailing list for several years but to see with my own eyes something of the work she was doing was amazing. Actually it would take many days to observe all the work of this ministry.

As the back cover of her book states:

> "From a humble beginning of a girl working out of her garage, nobody had envisaged that God would put his hand of blessing on the ministry of Christian Missions Charitable Trust and extend it to what we see today. The Haven of Hope Handicraft Centre that started in a garage, developed into CMCT – a ministry of faith and compassion to help the destitute, downtrodden, disadvantaged, and the poorest of the poor... impacted the lives of thousands who were rescued and restored by love and kindness."

It started when Colleen, who was still deep in language study, began to teach some local girls embroidery. They met in her garage. From this small group of half a dozen girls grew a ministry that reaches thousands of people. The varied works range from the care of lepers, a wheelchair project, a 24-hour pharmacy, eye hospital, physiotherapy unit, outreach to HIV patients, thirty five boys

---

7 Colleen Redit with Peggy Loh, (self published.)

and girls rallies (like club meetings) , ESOL classes, primary and secondary schools, HIV-effected women, a hospital, childrens sponsorship programme, industrial training for boys, three 'soup' kitchens in slums providing over 2,000 meals a day – and I'm sure I have missed some! They built 140 houses for people who lost their homes in the great tsunami of 2005 when 230,000 people perished in Asia including many in India..

Not only she helped large numbers of destitute people, she has adopted seven children and seen them grow and the older ones have married making a family of 15.

Colleen is not alone in the good works she does for the people. There are many Hindu families and groups with programmes to help the poor. But the difference is that the objective of this ministry to show the love of the living God.

It was during one of my visits to India that there was a ferocious argument going on as to whether Hindi be declared the official language of the country. The Southerners were strongly objecting to this, especially the Tamils, who were considered to be the most fluent. Then there were the augments as to the name of the main city of Tamil Nadu. Chennai was mentioned in the original deed issued to the first English settlers in August 1639, to Francis Day of the East India Company. Madras is a Telegu word and it was the name of a nearby fishing village. Others thought that it was a corruption of the Portuguese 'Mother of God.' It was finally settled in 1966. But to this day, people are divided with many still calling it Madras.

The city is famous for many things like being the oldest city corporation in the world after London. It has been included in one of the best 'food cities' by National Geographic. Chennai was also named the ninth-best cosmopolitan city in the world by Lonely Planet. In October 2017, Chennai was added to the UNESCO Creative Cities Network (UCCN) list for its rich musical tradition.[38] More than one-third of India's automobile industry being based in the city and is home to the Tamil film industry and major film production centre.

Who needs an introduction to Madras Curry? It is different to other curries in that it is spicier and served as mild, medium or hot, or as in New Zealand, Kiwi hot, which is halfway between medium and hot.

In pre-refrigeration days, there was a famous Ice House near the beach. Huge blocks of ice were brought from North America by sailing ship and stored in a specially built warehouse. "Frederick Tudor (1783–1864) sent ice on *Arabella* (696 tons), which made several trips from Boston to Bombay-Calcutta in 1853–1854, and each voyage lasted 150 days. *Young Mechanic* (1375 tons) carried ice to Madras in 1865, hired by Tudor, which on re-chartering in 1866 was lost to fire. The ships brought ice to Madras and carried back saltpetre, animal hides.

"Tudor packed huge ice blocks with generous insulations of wood shaving, sawdust, and rice chaff. Ice blocks were stacked tightly, approximately out of 180 tons of ice shipped, 100 tons arrived intact after travelling 25,000 km."

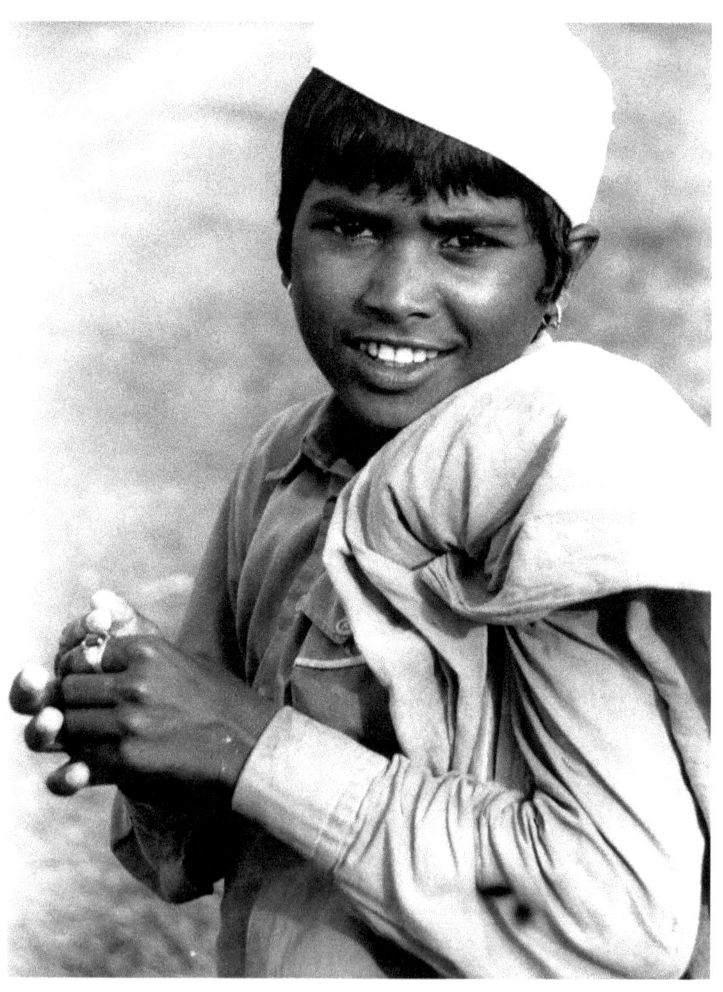

Gujarati boy.

CHAPTER THIRTEEN

COMPASSION INTERNATIONAL

For five years I was the director for South Asia of the American child sponsorship programme called Compassion International. I had 36,000 children all of whom came from the poorest of the poor. But sadly, the Indian government decided to forbid Christian foreign-based organisations from bringing money into the country as they considered it a form of evangelism and as such, an affront to Hinduism.

One tribe of people that lived in the forests of Orrisa had a most unusual custom. It was impolite to call out a person's name. When we had a meeting of the sponsored children and if I wanted to speak to someone, I would ask the person sitting next to her to tell her to come to me. Like 'Would the girl in the red blouse ask the one sitting next to her to please come to me.' Or 'I'd like to speak to the girl in the green blouse in the back row.'

It was my responsibility to see that the right children were being sponsored and that they were receiving all the help that had been provided for them by their sponsors. This meant travelling the country visiting the children. They were of the poorest of the poor. I had many unforgettable experiences doing this.

Like, sitting with a small family of four, two parents and two children, a boy and a girl aged seven and eight. Their place was in the compound of a warehouse and there were no people in sight. They were like unpaid custodians and were permitted to live there. This was in the outskirts of Bangalore. Early one evening I visited the family who had two sponsored children when they were preparing their one meal of the day. The had an old tin that would hold about two litres of water placed on a small fire of sticks. The father was placing tiny mice in it and boiling them into a soup. The soup was black. Most unappetising to me from the look of it, let alone what it contained. I noticed that he dropped the mice into the water without cleaning them. These six little mice would be their only protein of the day. They had a small quantity of rice – about two spoonfuls for each person. They welcomed me most warmly and offered me some. I declined, I hope graciously, and gave them a small packet of boiled sweets. When I wrote to the sponsors, I carefully omitted reference to the family's only protein of the day.

My colleague said later, 'It was nice that you gave them those sweets. They will probably never forget you. They will remember you for the rest of their lives – that's how special they were to them. I heard the mother say to the father in Kanada.' It would be true that they had never before received a European visitor to their tiny one room shack in which they all lived and slept together. The two primary school aged children were sponsored by an American couple and this enabled them to attend school, buy their supplies like books and uniforms, receive medical checks and treatment when required.

It was becoming dark but I could see that their 'house' was made of cleverly placed sheets of old plywood and roofing iron fastened together with wire. When I indicated that I would like to see inside, the mother quickly got to her feet and waved me in. It was about 10 feet square. The earth floor was swept clean and she quickly took a lamp made of a single wick in a small jar of kerosene and lit it from the fire. There were four nails in the wall from which hung each persons' clothes. They appeared to have one spare set each. The mother had a little English and said, pointing to her chest, 'Me nothing here,' pulling aside her sari to show me half of her breast. Then patting her hip said, 'Nothing.' Was that her subtle message to me to ask my wife to buy her some underclothes? There was a grass mat on the floor and she pointed to it and said, 'Everybody sleeping.' In one corner was a straw broom and an old wooden box which contained her cooking utensils like a few enamel plates, a large spoon, an ugly looking carving knife, some cracked porcelain cups and a couple of small stainless steel bowls. That was interesting to me because every Indian housewife in the country would have a set of stainless steel bowls.

A small a ledge on one wall had several books including a Kanada Bible and hymn books. Plus a few small bottles of medicines and a packet of Band Aids. The father of this little family went out every day looking for labouring jobs. He usually was 'lucky' several times a week.

One year when it was India's turn for a major audit by an international auditing company, I arranged to meet the auditor in Madras. This company gave us a free audit in one country every year. He was an American man on his first trip abroad. His young son had saved up his pocket money and asked his dad to give it to some poor children in India. He turned up a day late as his travel agent had got the time zones wrong.

After meeting him at the airport we checked into our hotel and he immediately wanted to go out on the street and find some poor children. 'My son will be anxious to know I've met some children.' I cautioned him to be careful and to wait until he could give the money privately. Within a minute of being on the street we were accosted by several street children. He immediately dug into his pocket for the money that we had already changed to Rupees. The kids crowded around him. He had ignored my advice so I kept walking leaving him to the mercy of those cute, dirty, smiling, ragamuffins. This was the best way for him to learn that he was not dealing with polite little Americans. Within seconds they had snatched his money and scampered down the street, leaving him, I think, deeply hurt and misunderstood.

Later at the office we presented him with a computer printout of our 14,000 sponsored children. As the auditor, he wanted to choose the ones he would visit. He picked a name, and the country director said, 'Ok but it will take us two days to reach him and you've only got ten here.'

'Never mind,' he said, 'we can fly there, that will be faster.'

'There's no planes to that place.'

'How do we get there?'

'We take a train, that's 23 hours, then two hours on a bus.'

'Ok then, let's do this one, pointing to a name.

'Sure but it's a full day to get there, if we're lucky.'

'What's luck got to do with it?'

'There's been flooding in the area so we might get held up for a day or two. But we can try. Last time I managed to hire a boat. However, if we have to overnight, there isn't any decent accommodation there.'

'What do you mean by that? I can pay for a hotel.'

'Ok, but be warned, the only hotel in the area has no beds, just mats on the floor. It only costs about one dollar and they don't take credit cards. We will take our own mosquito nets. But you'll get to try the local food. Its really good although usually a bit hot. He soon realised that 'a bit hot' was in reality, very, very hot. It will be easier if we take a taxi from the railway station instead of the bus, then we could be back in time to find a hotel. The return bus will not give us enough time to visit the kids.'

Our auditor was convinced that the boiled water in the hotel was quite ok, hadn't his travel agent told him so? Admittingly, a glass of cold water with several ice cubes is very appealing to an American. He completely ignored my advice of not drinking the water but only tea, coffee or soft drinks. This was before the introduction of good bottled water. But in the first village we visited he discovered the truth. He was interviewing a sponsored girl in her hut and asking her all the usual questions like, did she receive the birthday present money her sponsor had sent? But he was becoming uneasy, possibly I thought, because he was sitting on the dirt floor of the hut. After a few minutes I could see that he had become quite uncomfortable so I asked him if he wanted the toilet. Yes he did. He cut short the interview and awkwardly walked to the only one in the village. But it only had three walls around the hole in the ground with a dirty tin of water. He hesitated and asked if there was another one. Sorry, no. But go ahead, no one will be watching! I hoped he had taken my advice and carried some toilet tissue in his pocket!

Selecting the most needy children was always very difficult because of the great numbers. We always worked through churches and let the pastor or elders choose the children. I usually avoided being present when this was done otherwise I would have been mobbed by desperate mothers pleading for help. I did this only once and never forgot the way several mothers clad in the simplest of saris clambered around my legs, kissing my feet. There were several standing back with clinging young children and alternatively scowling at the others and calling 'Sahib, Sahib' holding up a child. I would privately tell a pastor that we could sponsor twenty children and suggest he select them, advising the mothers to come to the church to register the children without telling anyone. But word would get out and dozens would come to plead their case. It was heart-breaking to see the way a mother would hold up a scrawny child, fingering her stick-like limbs, thus demonstrating how great was their need of food.

He graciously gave us a good report on the quality of the work. He found nothing out of place and expressed his admiration of the way the staff went about their duties despite 'enormous difficulties.'

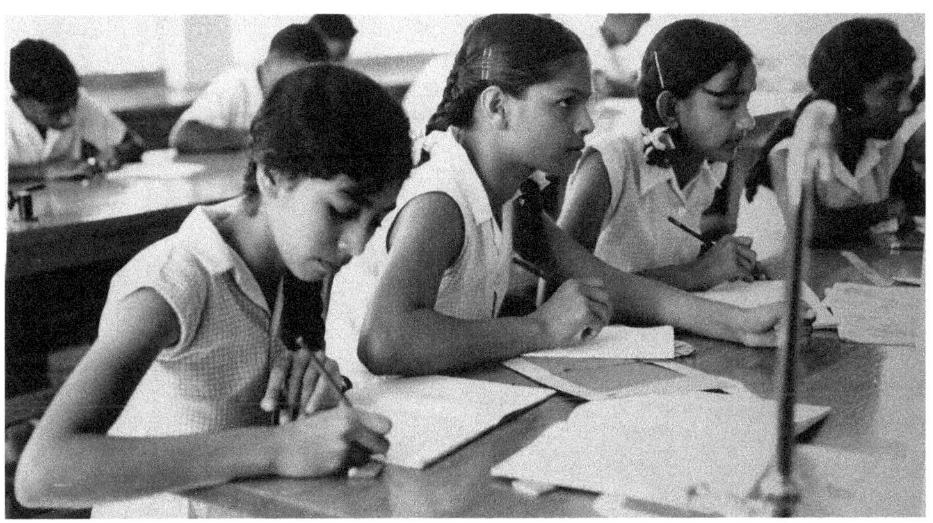

Indian school girls, Gospel Mission School, Suva, Fiji.

CHAPTER FOURTEEN

INDIAN RAILWAYS

The railways of India are an endless fascination. To say nothing of some notable maharajahs who built their own railways and even extensive model railways. The Maharajah of Gwalior is reported to have had a model railway that ran from the kitchen to the dining table transporting the food some 250 feet away. The system worked well until one evening during a dinner with several important people including the Viceroy, a wagon carrying a curry derailed and spilled its load into the laps of the chief guests.

Another version of the story:

> The Maharaja of Gwalior had a silver model train chugging along the centre piece on his banqueting table. Meant to circulate liqueurs and cigars to his royal guests, the train was operated at the touch of a button. The Maharaja was immensely proud of the show that his little toy train was put up at the end of every royal banquet. Alas ! One time the train derailed en route its tiny voyage. The Maharajas' rage knew no bounds. The servants quivered in their boots as the Maharaja ordered an inquiry to ascertain the reason behind the accident! History does not record the quantum of punishment handed out, if any.
>
> *Wikipedia.*

Only a few of the top trains have dining cars but the rest have a fascinating and very effective system of feeding the passengers. At a stop about an hour before lunch, a man gets on the train and takes orders. He hops off at the next station then telegraphs the orders to the station ahead. At the third station the food is brought aboard in stainless steel trays that have the food neatly set out in compartments of rice, dhal and various condiments. The standard meal is vegetarian but non-veg meals are available. At the next stop the trays are collected and payment made and taken off. I never had a poor-quality meal on a train.

On some express trains the assistant guard takes food orders and telegraphs them on ahead to the next station.

My local India manager knew of my interest in trains so decided instead of hiring the usual taxi we would go to a distant village by train. He sent an office boy on ahead to purchase the tickets and was given careful instructions as to what to get. Typical passenger trains in India had many classes, up to six and even sometimes eight. They are classified according to seating, sleeping and ventilation. A full description of all classes amounts to over 600 words.

There were no First-Class seats or bunks available, or air conditioned Second Class. At the rear of the train were a few Second-Class carriages with wooden seats. These used to be called Third Class but, in an attempt, to make them sound better they became 'economy non-ac seconds.'

We pushed and shoved our way aboard the last carriage, no 21, and found space on the floor. Most passenger trains have 20 to 22 carriages. The wooden seats, designed to carry three, had at least four or even five people jammed together. There would be about 1,800 passengers on this train. Our floor space was near an open door, so we had the benefit of a cooling breeze. But during the frequent stops the temperature shot up ten degrees, according to the tiny temperature gauge I carried. When stopped at one station I was amused to see the trolly of the permanent way inspector. It was four-manpower with the inspector seated on an armchair with an umbrella over his head. It was pushed along by four men, two at a time with the pushers running along the rail in bare feet. A noisy argument broke out between a seat of women and some young men opposite them. Latter my colleague explained that the women were castigating the young men for letting a white man, a visitor to their country, sit on the floor. Their response was simply, 'He's in India now.'

The *Continental Railway Journal* in December 1972 issued the following 'warning' to would-be travelling photographers, quoting someone who had who recently made a four-week tour of India using third-class rail travel, he wrote it was 'extremely arduous and mentally exhausting and consequently very disappointing…trains are often crowded so much so that it can sometimes physically impossible to climb aboard – and huge contingents of people travel on the roof.'

Here's another description by Anja in *Rail Across India.*[8]

> 'Until the crossing of the border of Uttar Pradesh things went right, but at the first station in Bihar it seemed as if total anarchy had broken loose. Together with all the others, our first-class compartment was overtaken by passengers who had either a 2nd class ticket or no ticket at all. In no time we were forty people sitting and lying on the benches and the floor, is a space that normally gives room for six persons. The corridors too were overloaded. With tooth and nail, we had to defend our seats, while in the meantime had become very cramped indeed. But still some people who were standing in the doorway, claimed that we were sitting like Maharajahs and there was room enough for some to sit between our feet and on our lap. We each ended up with two children on our lap and a woman seated on the floor between our legs. The ticket collector was of course too sensible to show his nose.'

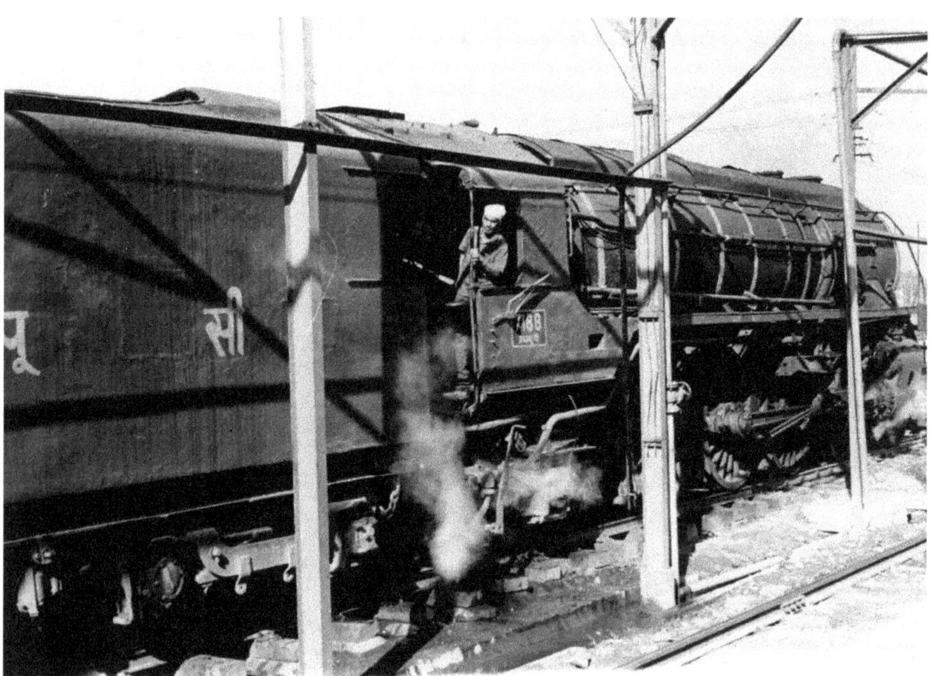

Indian Railways express locomotive.

8 *Rail Across India.* Abbeville Press.

The seventies and eighties were a steam enthusiast's delight with over 500 steam locomotives still in use. Many express trains were hauled by streamlined WP Pacifics. Altogether 755 were built in Canada, Poland and Austria with the last lot in India.

On some trains there is no way the train management can know the exact number of passengers. The number of tickets issued for a train is in many cases was quite irrelevant. When there is a serious crash the number of passengers are often completely unknown such as on 6 June 1981, a train in Bihar state derailed on the bridge across the Bagmati river and spilled into the river killing, according to the official statement, between 300 and 800 people! The one thing I disliked about Indian Railway carriages is the way it every window is fitted with bars – prevent people climbing in. But they also make it impossible to get out in a hurry or emergency.

Our tiny space was constantly being invaded by the legs and feet of others and it was with some relief that we disembarked at our destination after three hours of discomfort. I like the way one traveller accurately described being on a long distance passenger train.

> The train is plied by vendors and vagabonds of all kinds, at all hours. You can buy bracelets, batteries, or donate to a beggar, procure wristwatches, wicker-ware, a new wallet or mouthwash, invest in a cell phone, a bedsheet, a comb or a set of headphones, and purchase food ranging from bananas to biryani, eggs hardboiled or omelette, idli, vada, tomato soup, water or chocolate, soft drinks (but no booze.) Provided you have a few paisa, no one need starve on a train in India. Even a few cents will buy you a meal.

The train is a great place to meet people. They freely chat with fellow passengers often sharing food and drink. During that trip I have just described we were offered food by half a dozen people. My colleague, being aware of this possibility, had brought a large bag of sweets to pass around. I met one evangelist who told me that he does all his evangelising on a train. You can travel a hundred miles for a dollar. Fares are so cheap and he finds a ready-made audience everywhere he goes. I'm told that the caste system didn't always apply among people crushed together on a train. It is interesting to note that an Indian civil servant, Charles Trevelyan, told a House of Commons committee in 1853 that, 'railways will also be a great destroyer of caste, and the greatest missionary of all.'[9]

Most stations are crowded with people and not all of them are travellers. Some are quite dirty, rough places, frequented by the homeless, crippled and desperately poor. As soon as we stop the train is surrounded by people of all ages selling tea, samosas and all kinds of local fast foods like idilies and vadsas. As one fellow said, 'If the train is a street market, train platforms are street markets on speed.' Vendors have only minutes to sell many cups of chai, samosas, idlies and vadas. Idlies as described by a famous American-Indian cook Vaishali, as *'delicate, fluffy, moon-like lumps of steamed, south Indian style lentil and rice cakes-are not just fun to eat, they are fat-free, full of protein, and really great for you.'* While vadas can be either fritters, cutlets, doughnuts, or dumplings. Ideal as snacks during a train journey.

I often tried to find a reason and the time to travel on the longest rail journey – from Delhi to Madras – 1,294 miles or 2,185 km – a 40 hour marathon. Bombay to Calcutta was also tempting – 36 hours, 1,223 miles or 1,968 km.

Here's a grim statistic – As many as 49,790 people died on railway tracks after being hit by trains nationwide between 2015 and 2017, according to this reply to the Lok Sabha (Parliament's lower house) on July 18, 2018. The Minister of Railways went on to say that nowadays a common problem is the use of mobile phones and other electronic gadgets while crossing railway tracks.

The largest employer in India with 1.4 million employees is Indian Railways. It is one of the largest railways in the world with over 115,000km of track over a route of 65,808km and 7,112 stations, with freight and passenger revenues of US$24 billion. Rolling stock includes 10,499 locomotives and 66,392 passenger coaches.

Someone once said that the domestic airline once known as India Air, was Indian Railways in the sky – or was it the other way around! The railways run 11,000 trains carrying a staggering 23 million passengers a day – sounds a bit like an airline.

People like me who come from such a small country have difficulty in imagining such a vast country that is about 27 times larger than my own!

---

9 Lawrence James, *Raj*, Little, Brown and Company.

I was talking to an evangelist in Chennai who told me that he did most of his evangelising on trains. 'We can travel for hours for a dollar and travelling people are always ready to talk, no matter what their caste.' I heard that from men like him. I had a spare day so he invited me to spend a day on the train with him. I bought two 'second non a.c.' tickets so that mean it would be a hot trip on hard wooden seats. We met on the platform and while we waited for our train, he bought some food and sweets. When he saw me look at them quizzically he said, 'it's not all for us. It is important to have some to give away.'

Strangely, the train was not as crowded as usual and we soon had a full bench seat to ourselves. Opposite us were three young men and a young woman. During the two-hour trip the evangelist conversed with the men and found that they and all been to mission schools but didn't have a clear knowledge of the Gospel. They soon heard it from my friend. The young woman sat quietly and never said a word. It was a local train and when we reached the destination we parted company with the three young fellows assuring us that they would get in touch with a pastor in their village. They were each given a Bible Society Gospel pack that had the *Gospel of Mark* and several leaflets about various subjects. But the young woman quietly said,' Please may we have a private discussion?' We found a few seats in a quieter part of the station, but with the evangelist saying that it was important to stay out in the open with her. Not that there are many quiet spots in a railway station in this country. After taking a cup of tea she commenced her story.

I am Johanna , I'm 31 single, no kids, never been married. But hoping that someday I'm going to walk down the aisle with the man that will truly love me for a life time.' I come from a broken family which means there were no parents since my birth to look after me. I was left under the custody of my grandmother, aunts and uncles, and when I grew older I learned to stand on my own feet. I had to survive the daily life. But in my own ways, I still give back help to my relatives as a sign of being so thankful for taking care of me while I was I growing up.

I have Japanese blood. My father was a pure Japanese but sad to say I never seen him as his contract here finished before I could see him. There's no photo of him so I have no idea what he looked like.

Nobody wants to be lied to and cheated. But when I was young and open to all about my life, I was molested by two different men. One was my uncle and the other was my uncle's church worker who is the brother of my uncle's wife. I was only thirteen when this man invited me to his home to meet his wife. But she wasn't there so he showed me his bedroom and told me to lie down on the bed and have a rest. Its true I was tired as I had walked a long way. He lay down beside me and began to lovingly touch and fondle me. I didn't understand. I thought it he was being loving and kind. I was wearing a long skirt and no panties because I was not old enough to have a sari. I don't need to say any more except that he raped me. Even then I didn't understand what was happening, only that it hurt a lot.

About three weeks later the church worker called to visit us but I was the only one at home. I don't think I need to tell you all the details, but he cleverly seduced and raped me. Again, at first, I thought he was being very kind to me by offering some Bengali sweets and some Rupees. He even suggested I go to live at his place and be their servant. But after the rape, I never wanted to see him again.

My big problem was that I didn't know anyone I could talk to about this. My relatives never spent any time with me or want to chat. All of the cousins despised me because I was illegit and not a pure-blood Indian.

Life was very tough during my growing up years so I had to fight against the everything and not let it traumatise me. But I always had some trust issues about men. So I managed to stay away from anything I didn't understand. But the time came when I felt overcome by depression. So I began to open up my heart again and found a boyfriend. But he betrayed me. I went to his house and found him in the bed with another girl. So he was the very last man that I had a relation with. He was a liar and a cheater because I found out that he had being seeing this other woman for two years. I think you call that two-timing.

I cried and prayed that hopefully, he was last man in my life. Except, when I will fall in love the man who is going to my partner and husband, that is according to God's will. And that he will marry me and love me with all his heart.

Later the evangelist commented on the way this woman had been so frank with her story. It is a most unusual thing in India. Women have to be very careful not to be seen by a man not of her family. Their reputation is easily ruined. But I think it is the men who are to blame for this. They can't be trusted. You see knowing who we were, she trusted us. That trust must be carefully preserved.

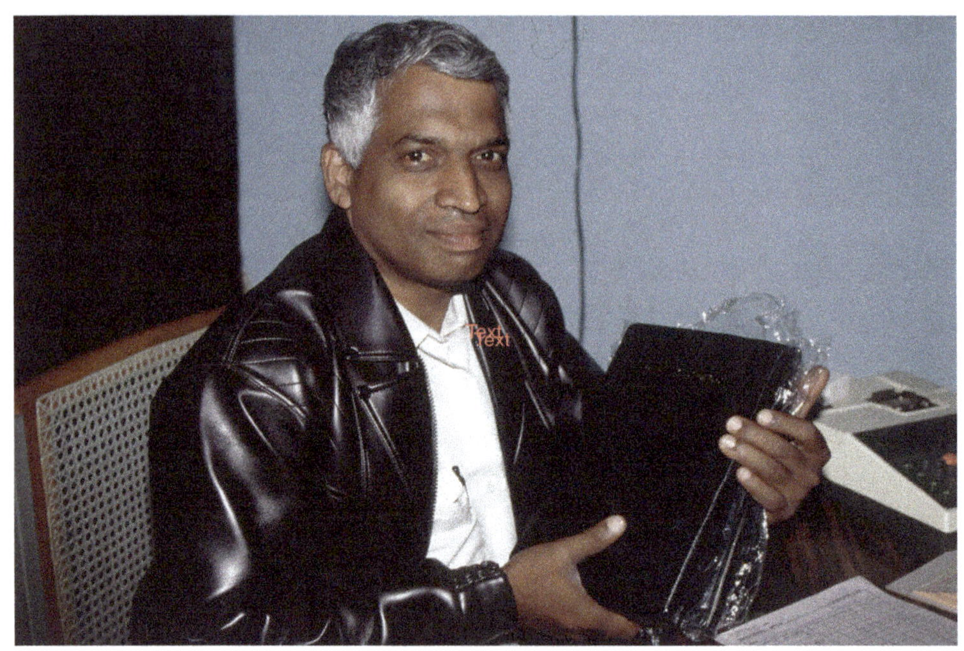

Malayali man with Malayalam Bible.

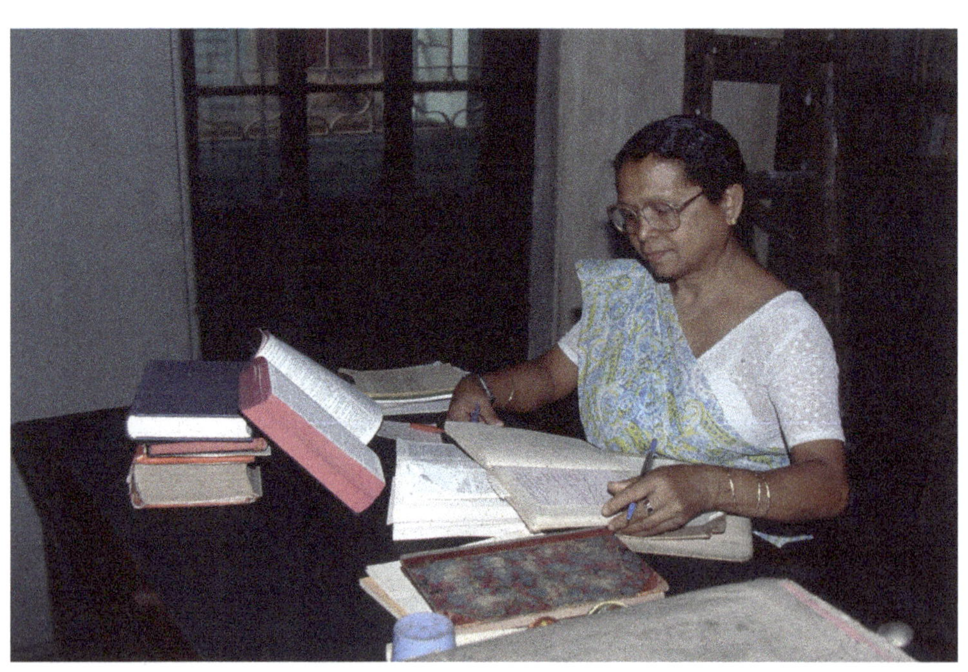

Bengali Bible translator.

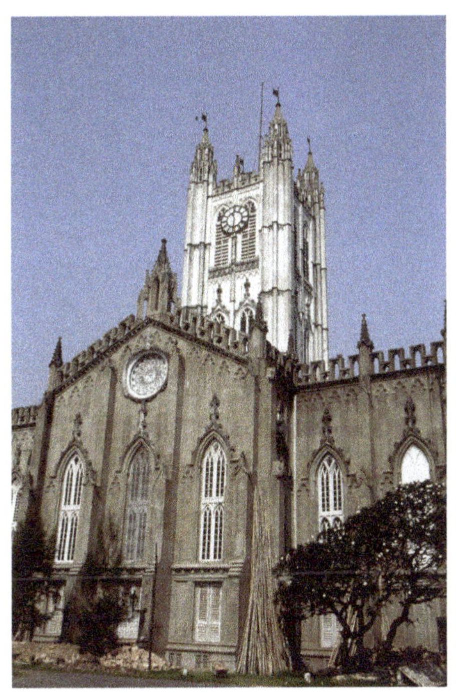

English church cathedral, South India.

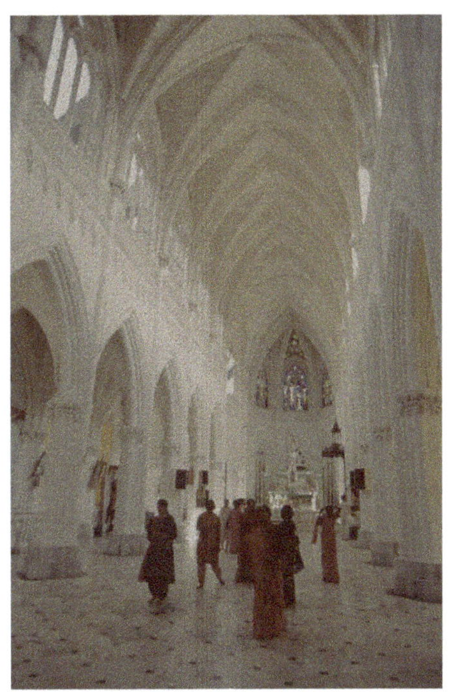

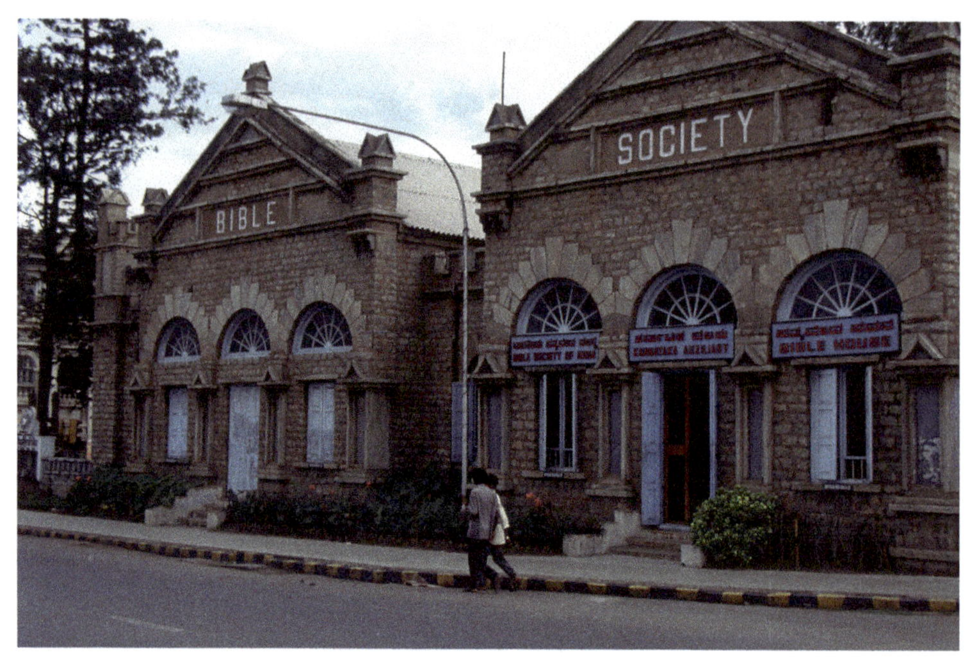

1902 Bible House, Bangalore.

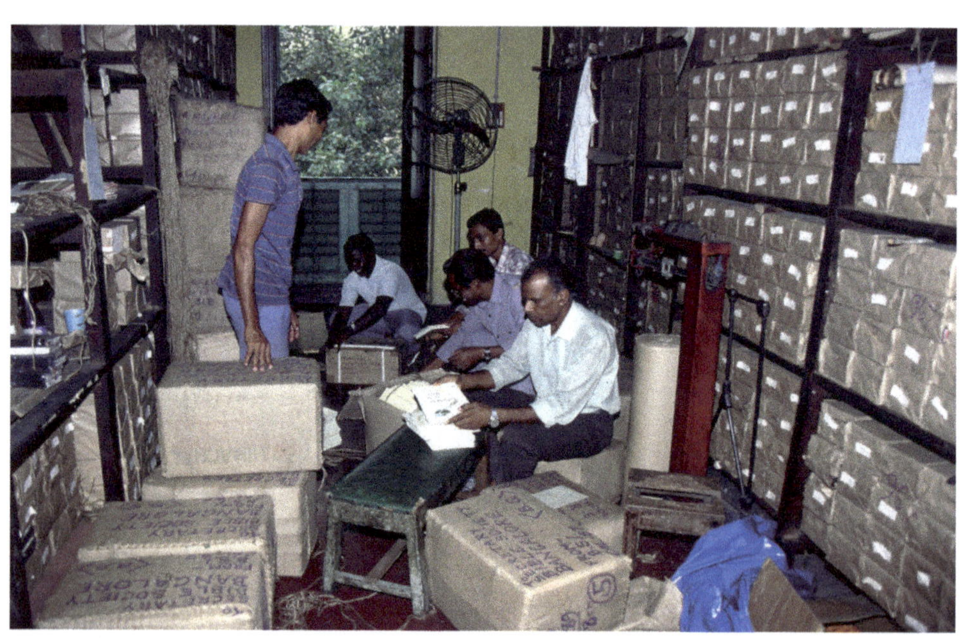

The Bible Society India uses more paper than the government.

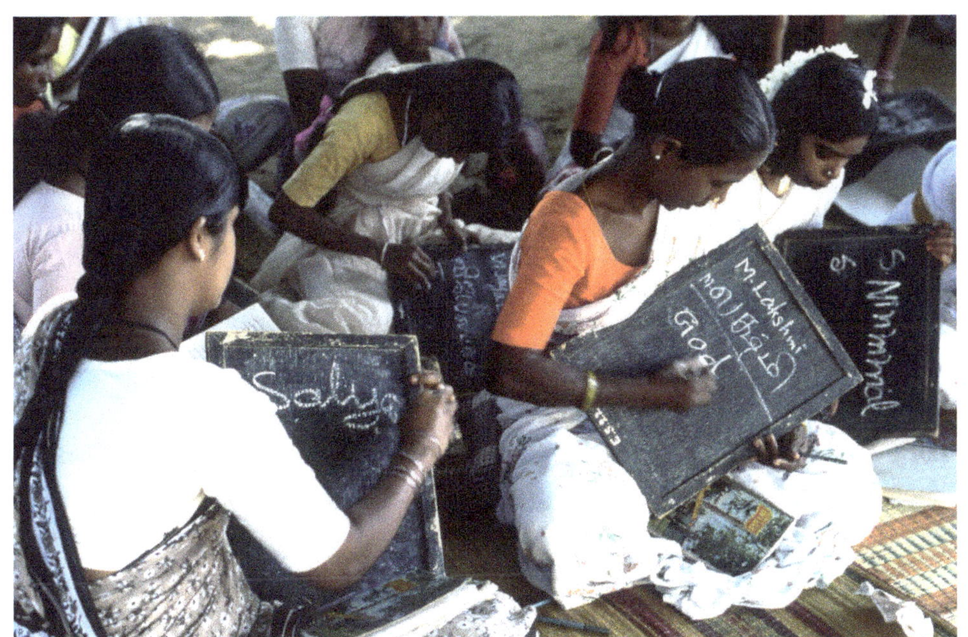

Literacy class.

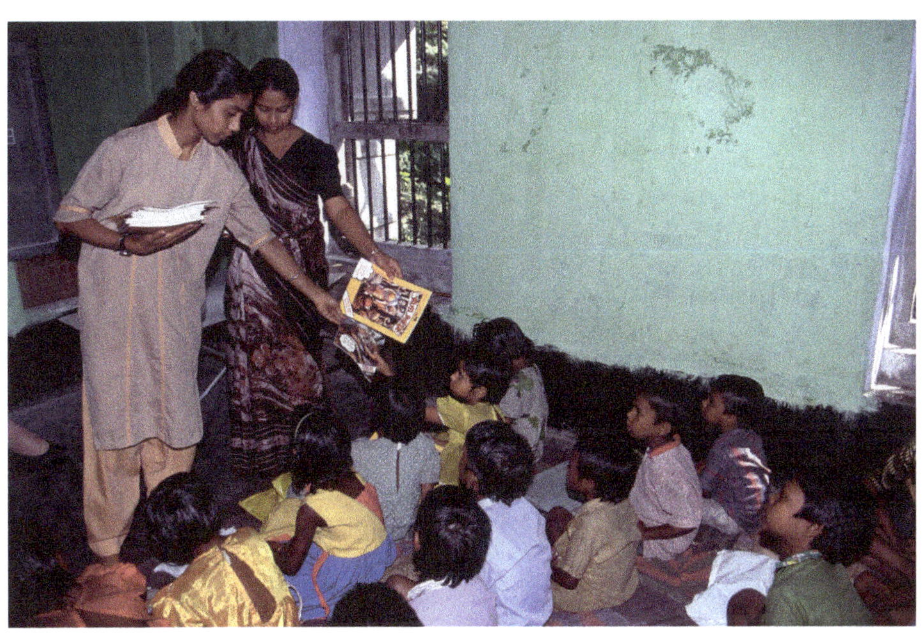

Great efforts made in education.

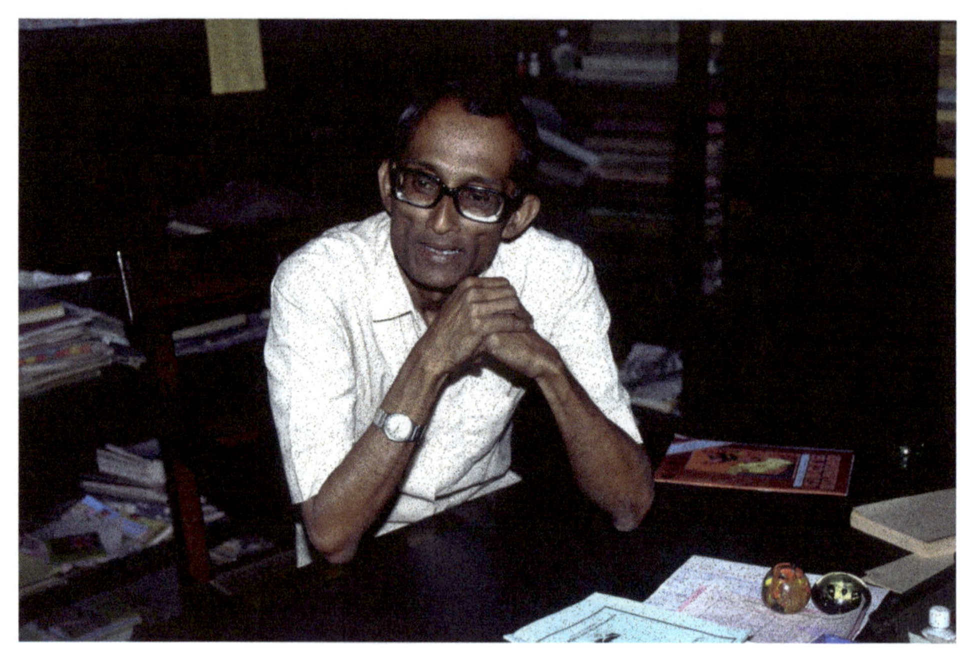

Bengali man.

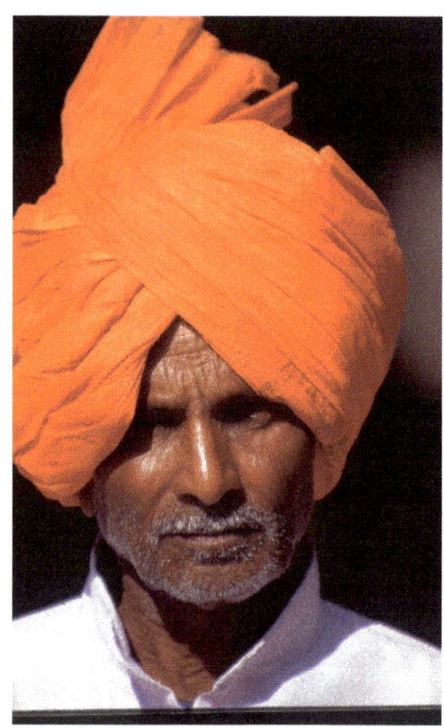

Rajasthan elder.

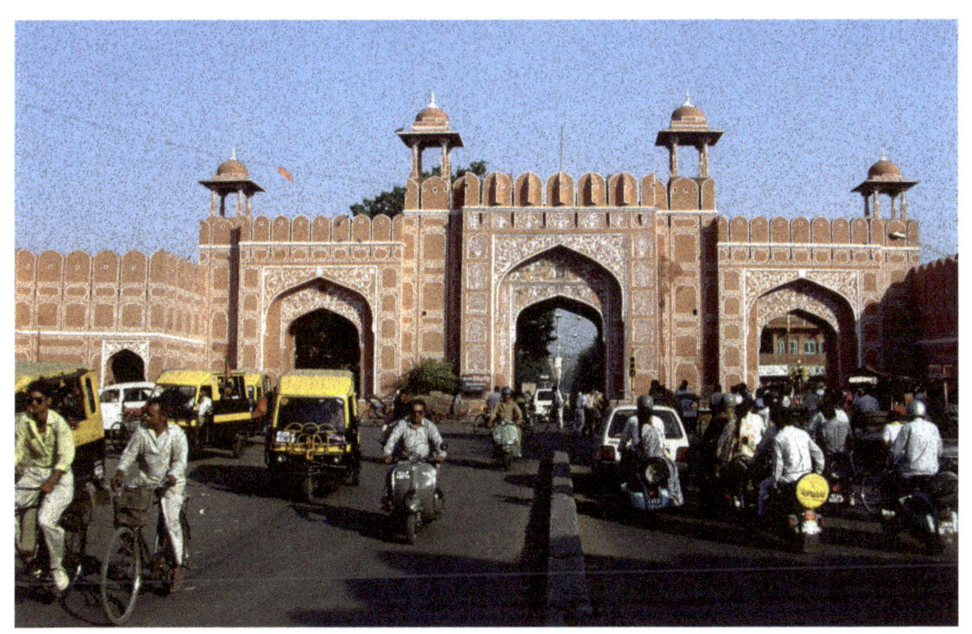

Mughal architecture, Agra.

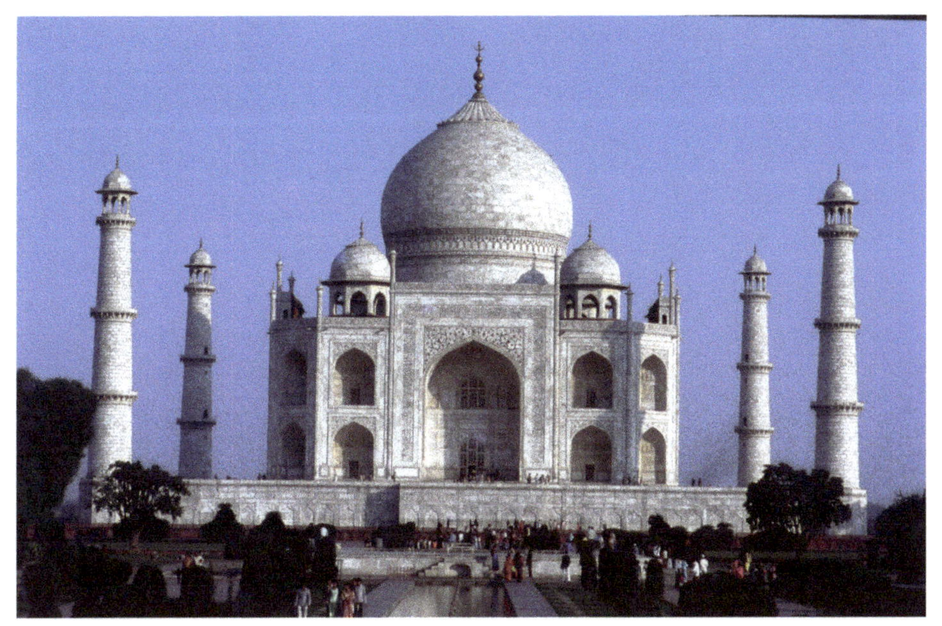

Taj Mahal, Agra.

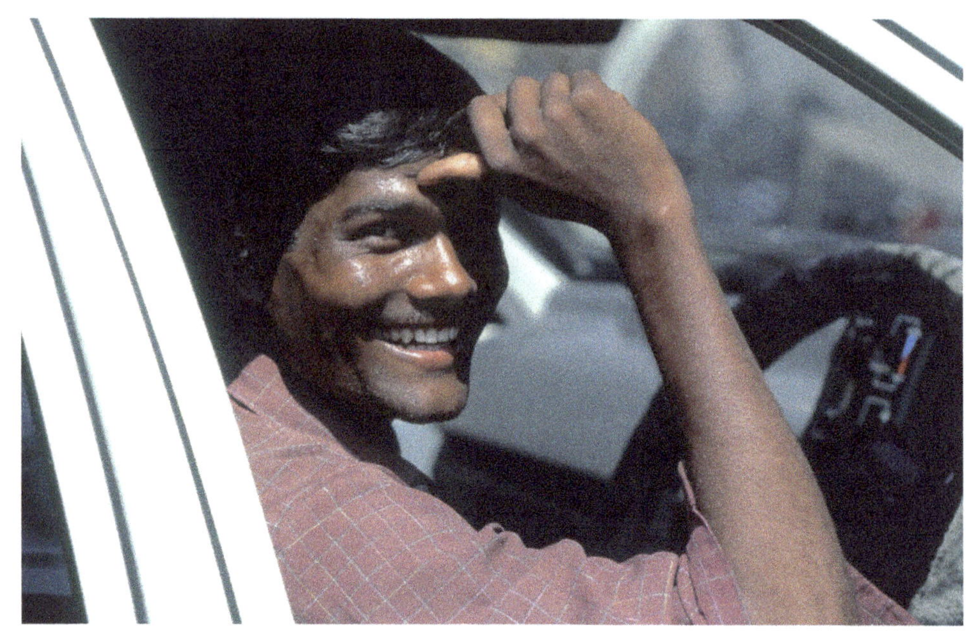

Taxi driver, Bombay.

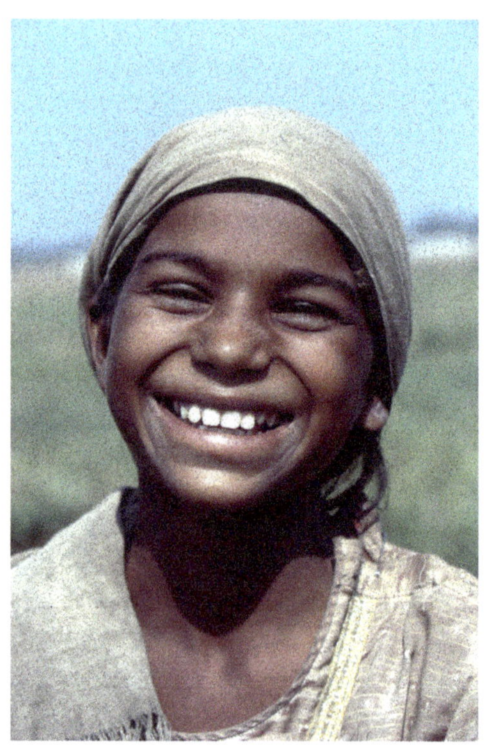

Gujarati village boy.

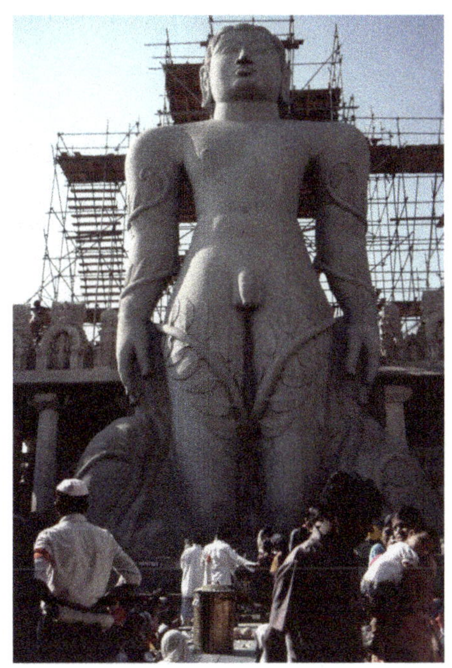

57 ft Gommateshwara statue, Karnataka.

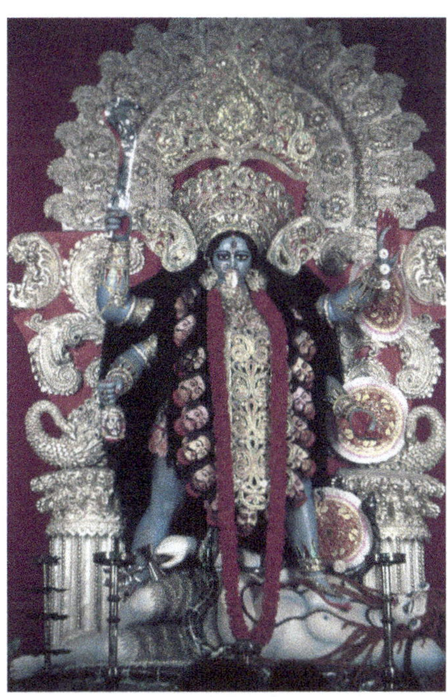

Hindu Kali festival, Kolkata

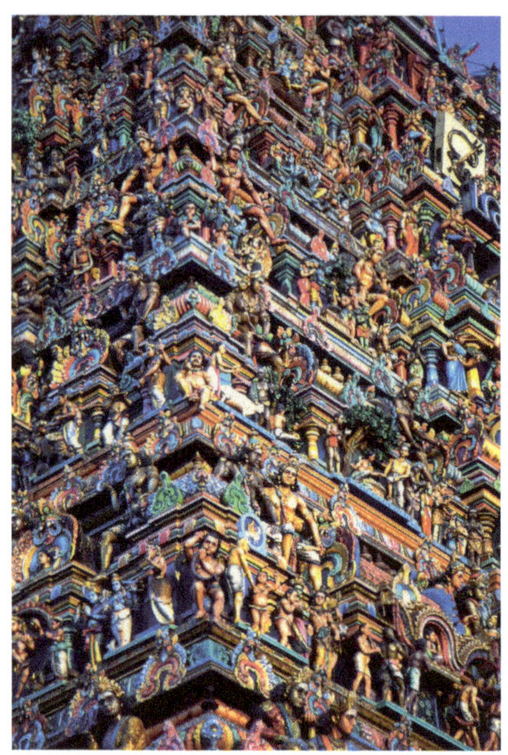

Temple, Tamil Nadu.

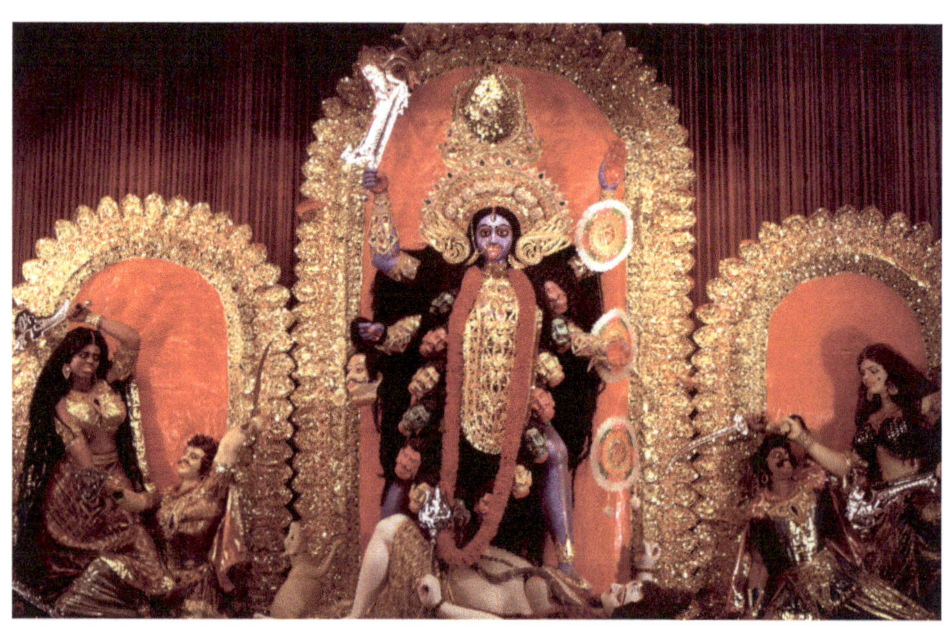

Hindu goddess.

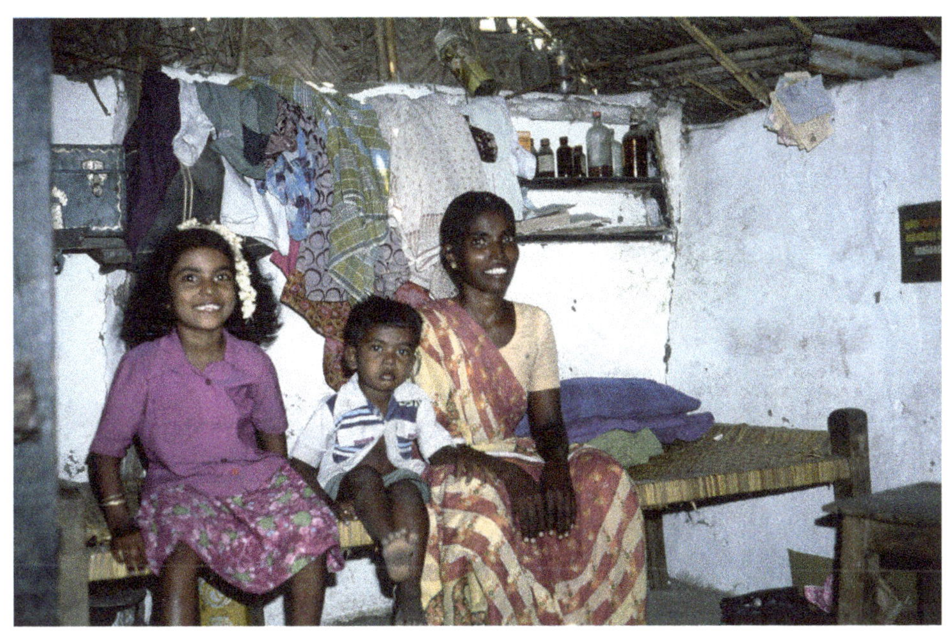

Widow and children sponsored by Compassion Int.

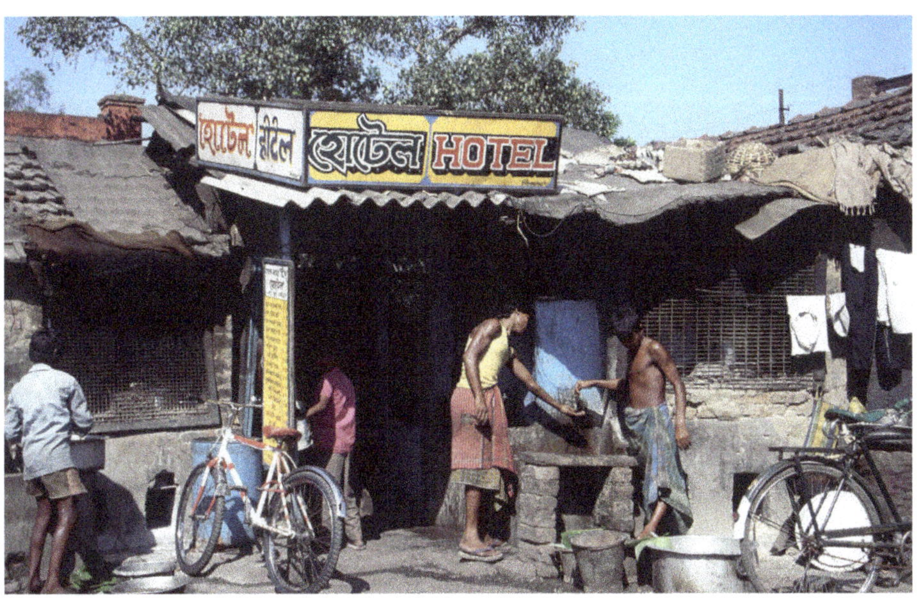

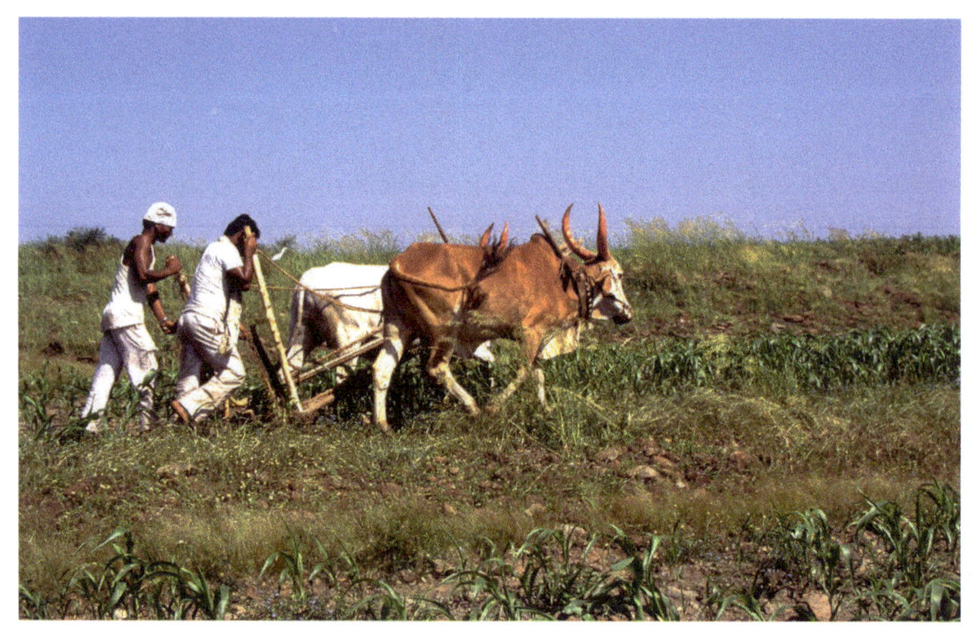

Ancient yet modern plough.

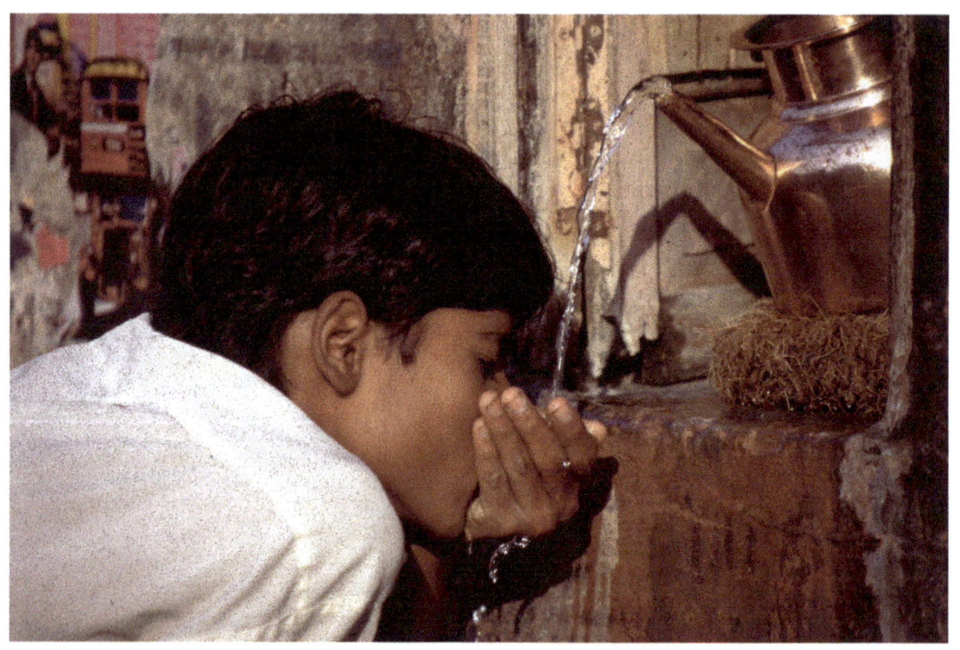

Life giving water.

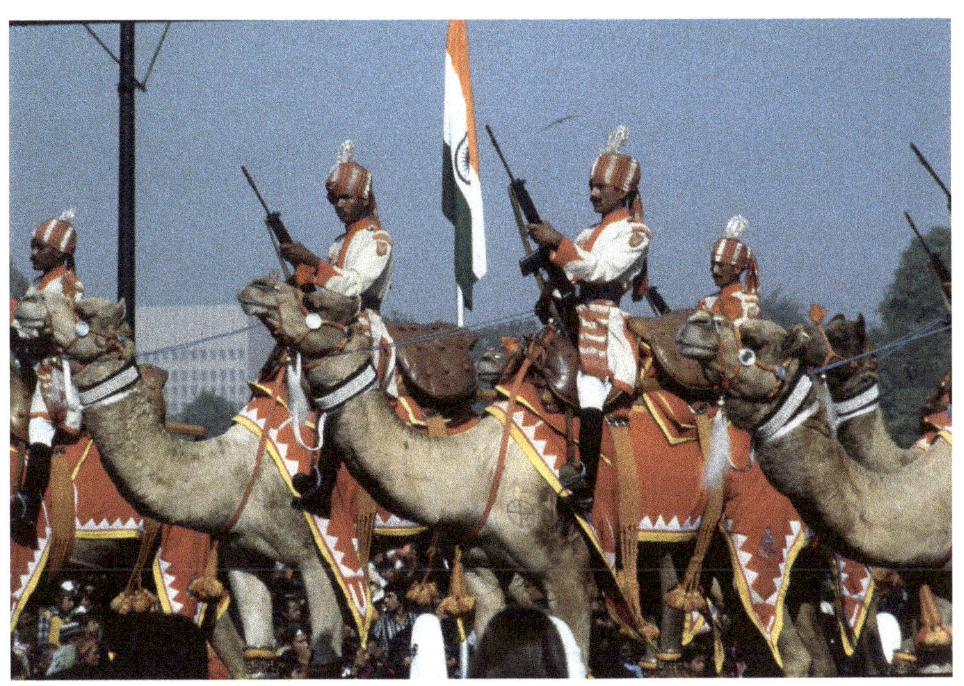

Camel Brigade India independence celebrations.

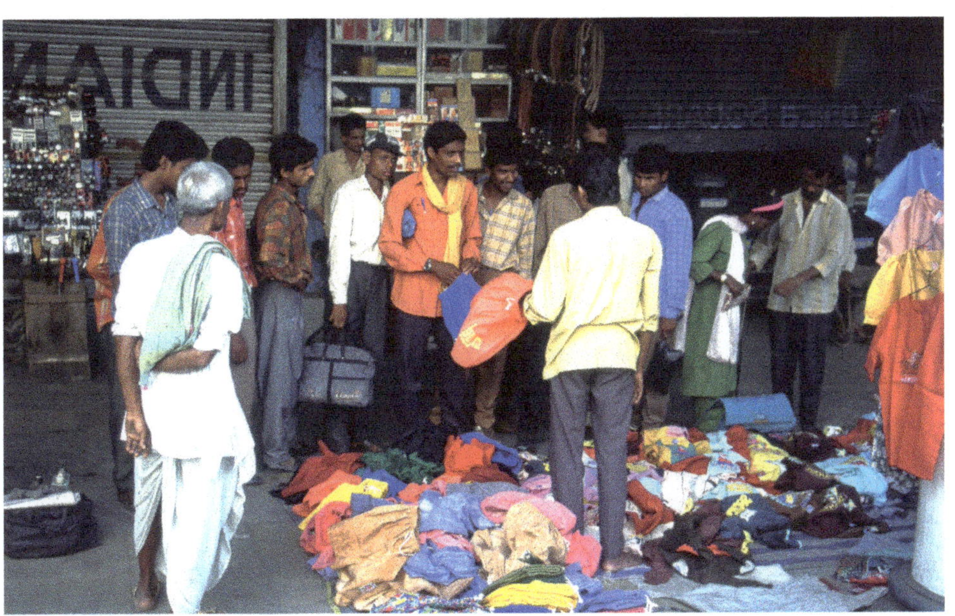

Street market.

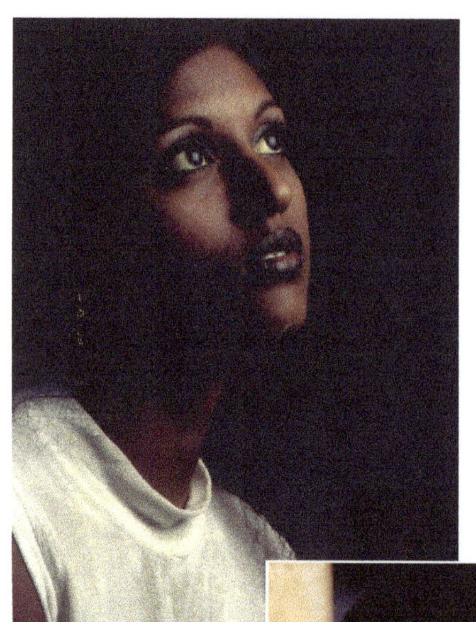

An illustration of the diaspora - three girls in three countries - Zambia, New Zealand and Singapore.

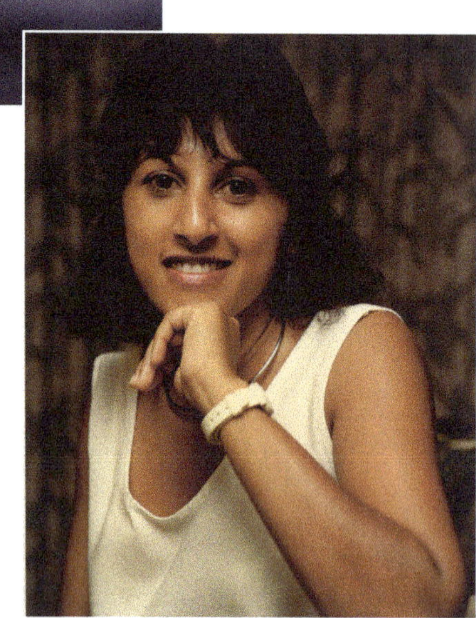

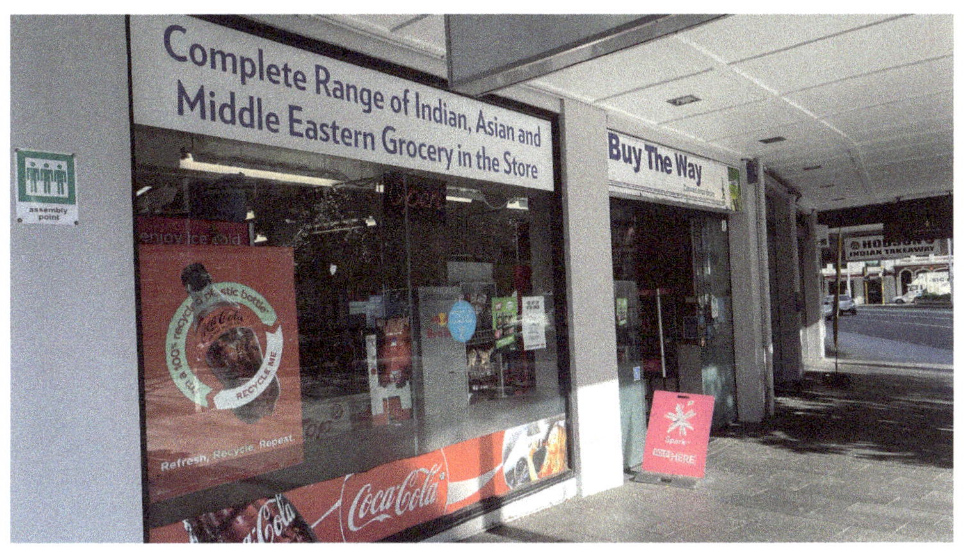

Indian-owned convenience store, Auckland.

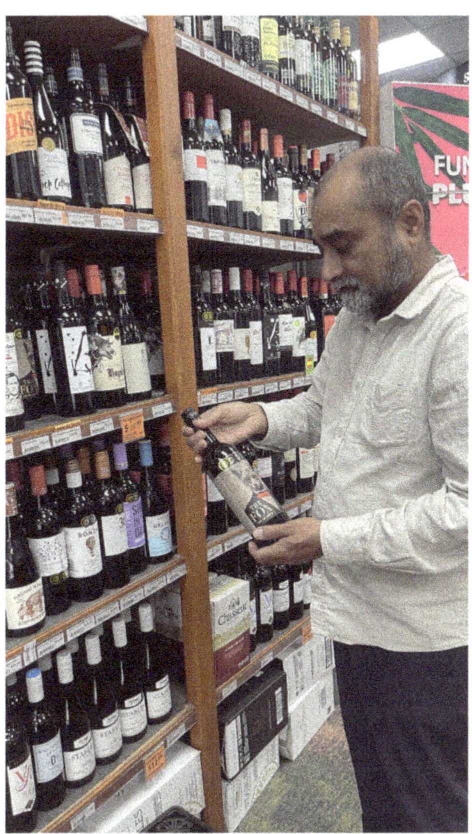
Vashishth, Gujarati businessman.

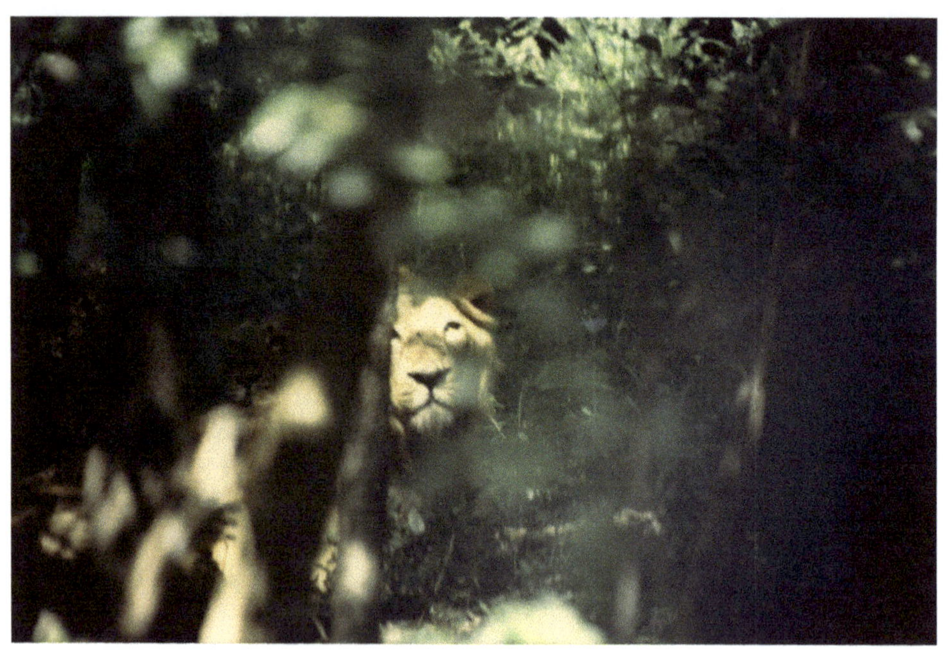

Rare photos of Asiatic Lions, Karnataka.

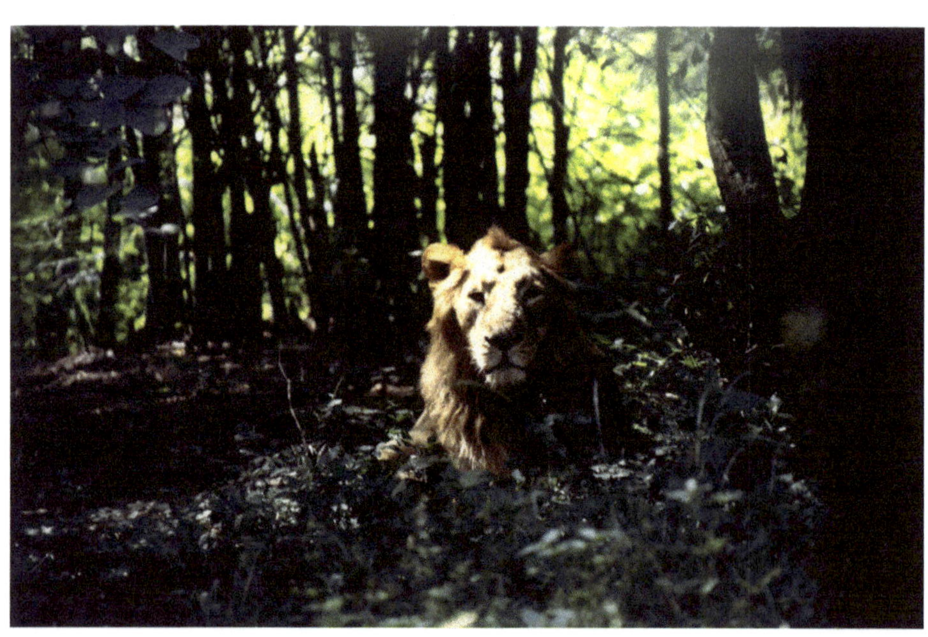

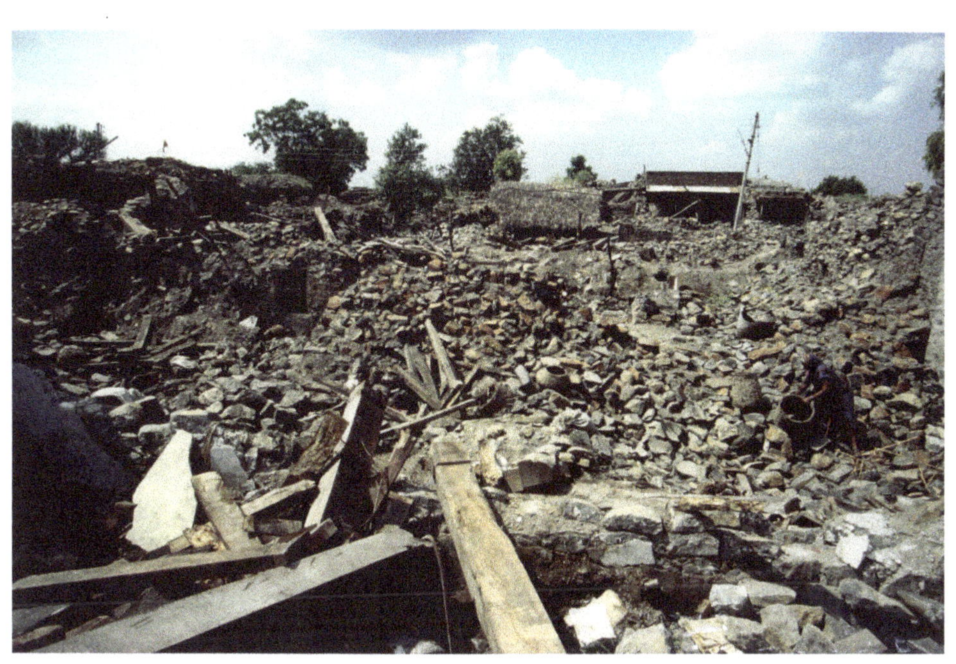

Devastation of Gujarat earthquake.

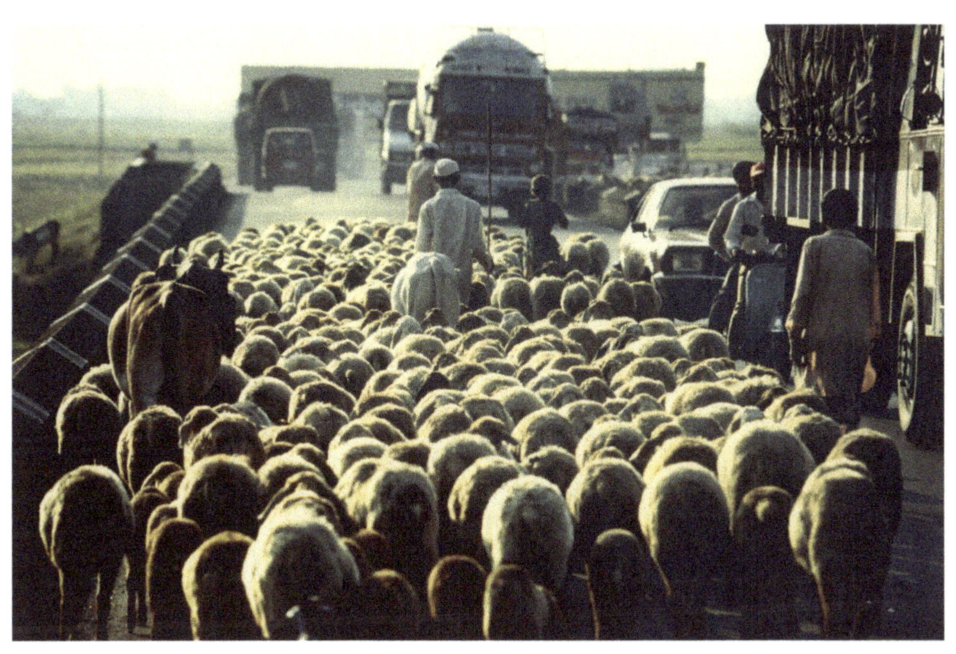

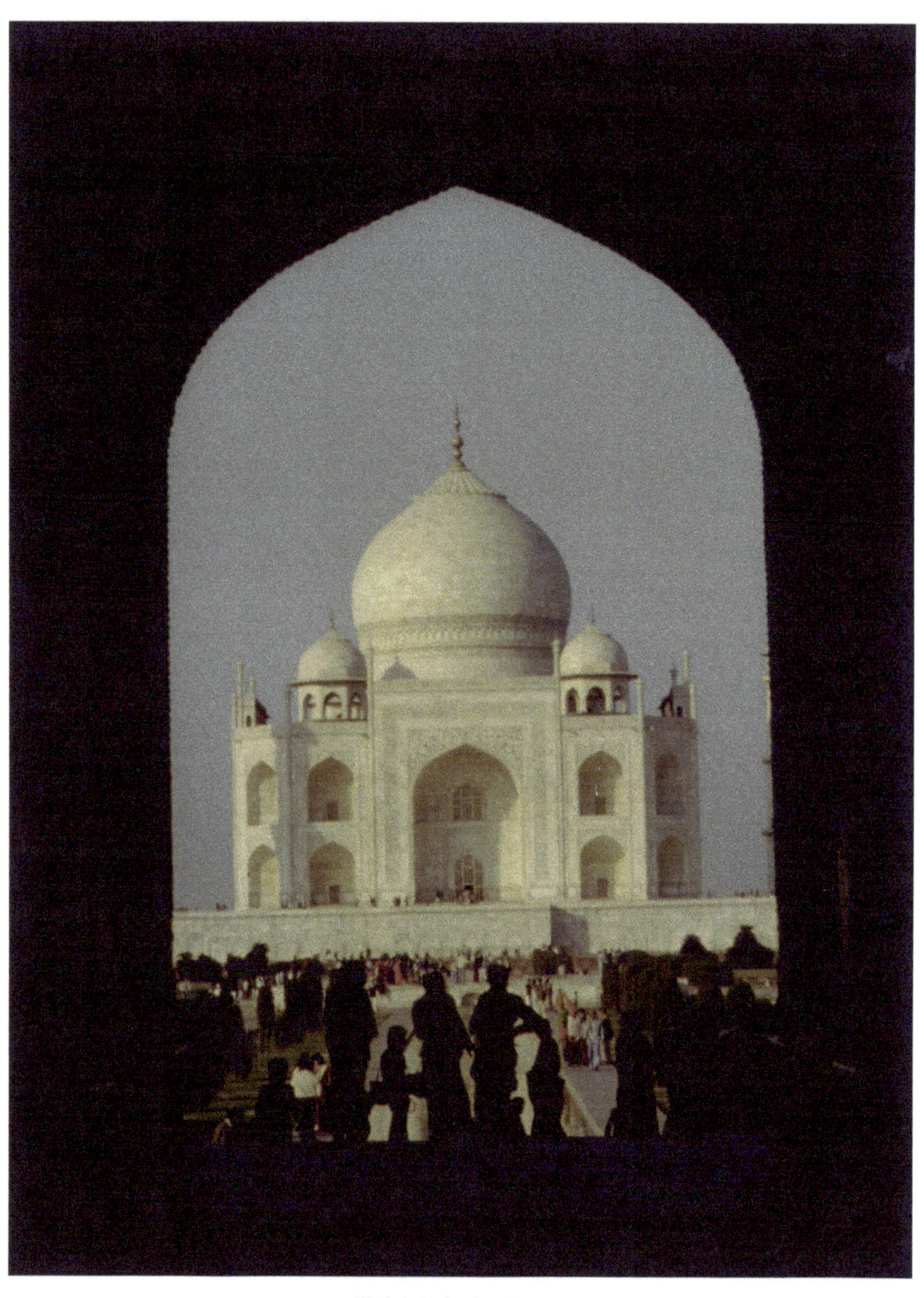

Taj Mahal, Agra.

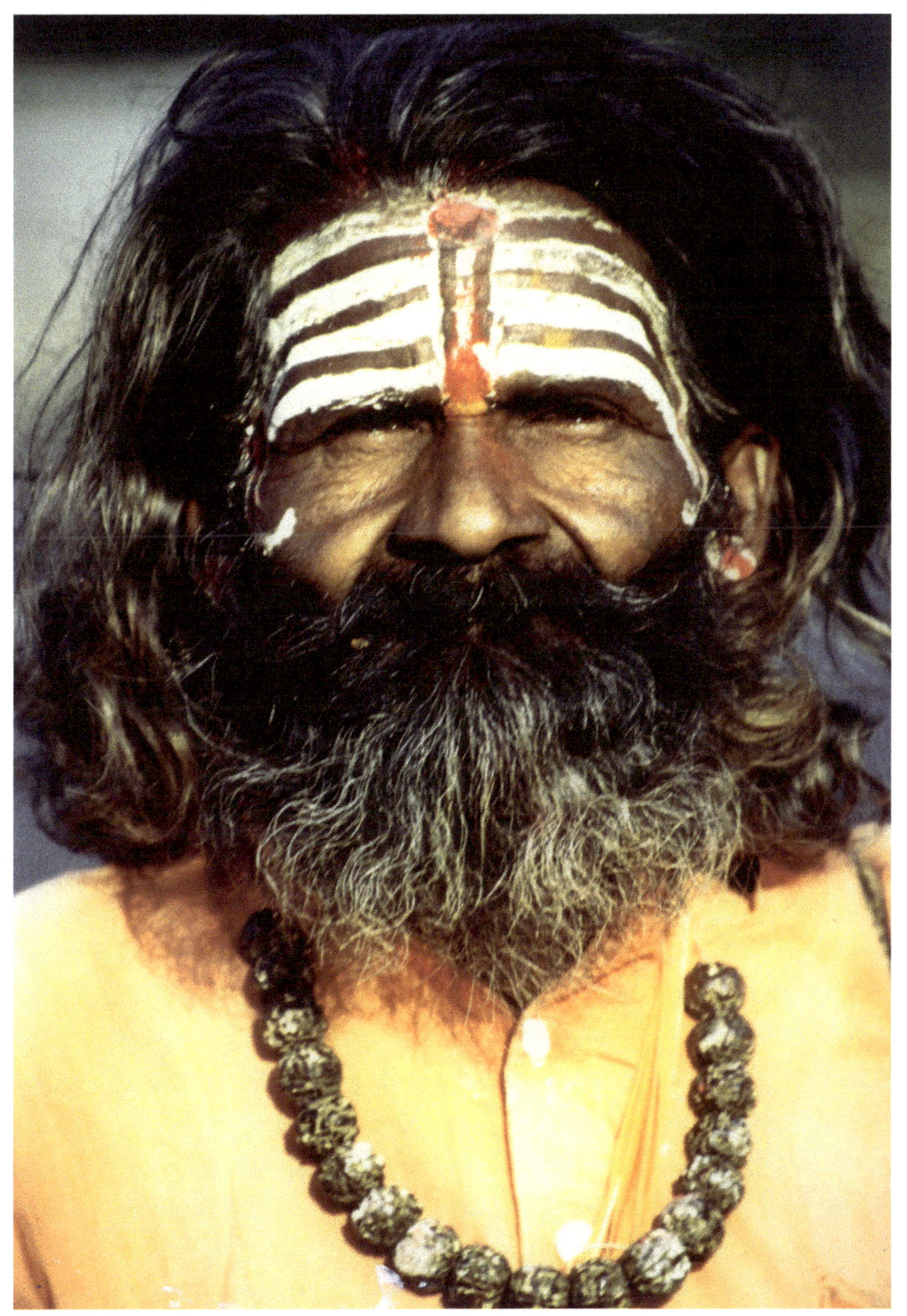

Hindu holy man.

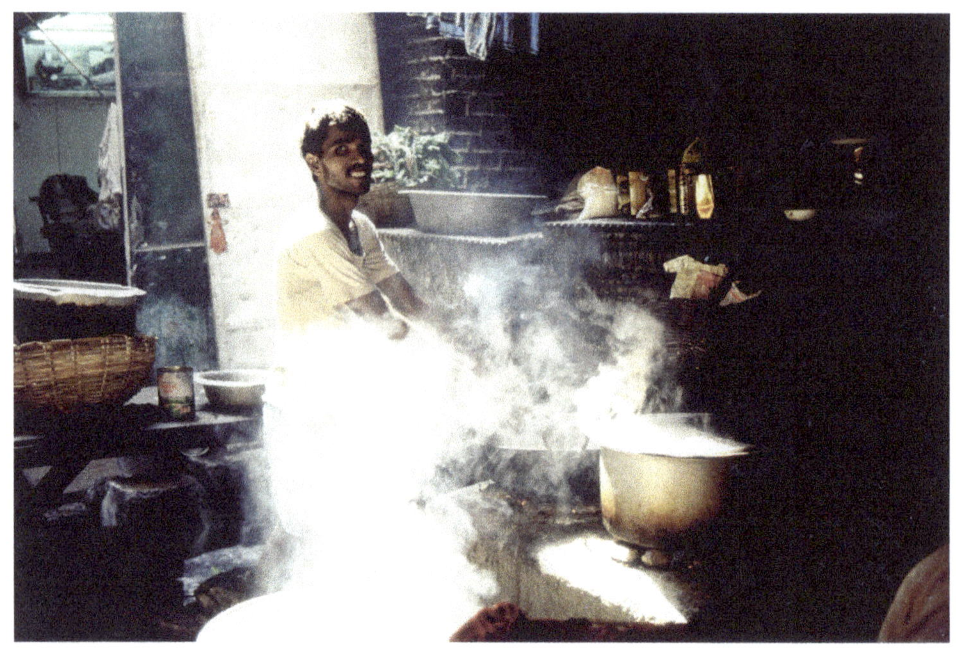

Tea shop Kolkata market.

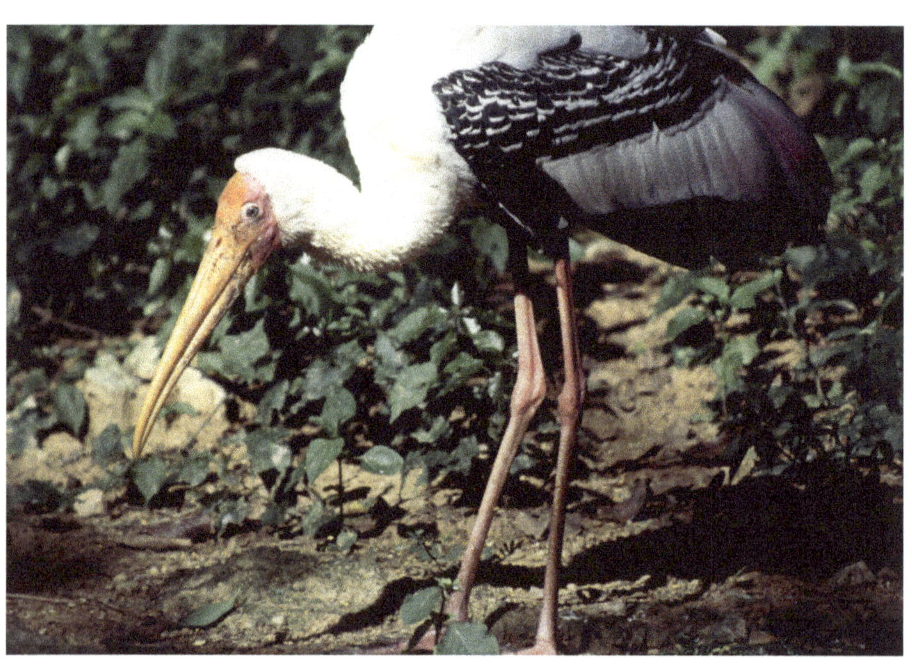

CHAPTER FIFTEEN

ALLAHABAD

'The city of God' Allah (god) abad (city), Allahabad, reminds me of one time when I flew there from Bombay. My travel agent had booked me on the last flight and when I saw this, changed it to the second-to-last. If there were delays, then usually the last flight is cancelled. The last flight that day crashed killing everyone on board. The aircraft had been scheduled to fly to Madras but it was switched to the Allahabad flight. A Boeing aircraft was originally supposed to make the flight but developed engine trouble and was replaced with a Sud Aviation Caravelle. Shortly after take-off the No. 2 engine failed. The crew immediately turned back to attempt an emergency landing on Bombay Airport's runway 09. But a thousand yards short of the runway, the pilot lost control and they plummeted to the ground killing all 171 people on board. It wasn't until the next day that I suddenly thought that I had better let them know at home that I changed my flight and was safe!

The other memory of Allahabad concerned my host. As he was driving me from the airport he suffered a heart attack. So I had to move him across to the passenger's side of the front bench seat and drive him to the nearest doctor. He faintly gave me directions and happily, after a few days, made a good recovery. Next day I received an urgent call from the head office in Bangalore asking how I was as they had heard I had suffered a heart attack! Thankfully, it wasn't me.

On 13/7/1987. Clive was returning to his school in Switzerland and my flight to Delhi was close to his check-in time, so we had breakfast together at the airport. I had heard about severe unrest in Delhi, but I never told him. Neither had I told Lorraine. There was no point in alarming them because one can usually avoid trouble spots. As a colleague in Beirut said to me during their civil war, 'If there's trouble down one street then go down the other!'

I was to take a two-day marketing workshop for the Madras field staff then; the plan was to return to Delhi and go on to Allahabad as the diary notes, "I'm at the airport in Madras now and the flight has been delayed 30 minutes, so we won't leave until after 10 pm. I hope the strike is finished in Delhi. There have been more fatalities in Delhi that day." I stayed at the hotel near the railway station. The city was very quiet.

When I arrived in Delhi at 12.30am there had been a good deal of tension in the area. I stayed at the Sheraton Hotel in a quiet part of the city. About fifty people had been killed and a curfew imposed. However, despite the fact that I arrived at midnight they had taxis and hotels operating for tourists. My driver drove cautiously through the deserted dark streets that are usually thronged with people at all hours of the day or night. I stayed in the hotel all day because of an unusual day-long curfew. It wasn't safe to go out before taking the train to Allahabad. I had special permission from the police to go the railway station. Again, the city was eerily quiet.

The train to Allahabad in North India, was about an eight-hour journey. I had a seat in a second-class air-conditioned coach. The a.c. worked well despite the outside temperature of 42C. There was an unusual atmosphere in the carriage as people breathed a sigh of relief to be away from the city where there had been so much unrest. They openly discussed the number of fatalities and generally agreed that the government figures and the newspapers were wide of the mark. Officially there were 16 people killed. A couple of Sikh men declared the number to be closer to 100. One, with tears streaming from his eyes and into his beard said, "They killed a whole family of my neighbours. All six of them. It was terrible, they just entered the house pulled the two men outside and killed them with swords and knives stabbing them again and again. Their blood is still on the footpath. They brought out the men first leaving their four women screaming inside the house as they were being raped. Then they dragged them outside onto the street almost naked and stabbed them to death. Then they cut off their breasts and threw them to the dogs. We called some friends to come and take care of the four young children."

But thankfully it was nothing like the Sikh massacres that had happened three years ago when thousands had been killed after the Prime Minister's Sikh bodyguards had killed her. Next day there was terrible revenge taken against the Sikh population when about 3,000 were killed in Delhi and about 20,000 in other cities.

Because I was a Christian worker, I often met people who wanted a blessing or counsel. This was requested in different ways, like touching my feet or standing bowed. Mothers would sometimes bring a child for a blessing. Touching the head and saying a prayer was all they expected. For some reason, staff in Allahabad at the office of the Bible Society considered me a counsellor. Often someone would quietly speak to me about some problem. One morning a senior secretary, Sunita, asked me to meet her after work and hear her story. Noticing that she was wearing a wedding ring, I said, 'Sure, come to my hotel tonight and bring your husband too.'

The hotel reception called me and announced visitors had arrived. When I went to meet them I was surprised that it was three women. No sign of the husband. 'Sorry, he has an engagement and can't come, so he sent his two sisters instead.'

I looked around, wondering where we could sit and talk. Sunita said, 'It's ok if we all come to your room because there we can talk privately.' So I ordered tea and snacks and led them upstairs.

We had no sooner seated when Sunita began her story. My story is so sad because when my mother was nine years old, she had an accident when she knocked over a gasoline lamp, and it burned her stomach and the left side of her hand. My grandmother took her to the hospital. A blood transfusion was needed but my grandmother did not have money. The AB-type was so expensive. There was a man who offered a free blood bag to my grandmother and it was type AB. But the problem was that he was a crazy man. My grandma accepted that offer even though the owner was mentally disabled. But it saved the life of my mother.

But my mother was not a normal girl and had a mental problem that by the time she was 10, she acted like a little child. But when she was 15 years old and nicely mature, her step-father raped her. Her young siblings saw it happening, and they tried to tell the grandmother what they saw their father do to my mom. But she said their father could not do that to their sister and admonished them for telling lies.

Mother was raped several times a week by her step-father for over a year. When she complained to her mother, she would not believe it because she thought my mother, having a mental problem, was just imagining it. But later, my mother tried to escape from their house and from her step-father because he was always attempting to rape her. She said that sometimes she enjoyed it, but other times he hurt her.

After a year, mom became pregnant by her step-father so my grandmother transferred her to a place far away where no one knew us. She gave her to relatives in Bombay. Life was so tough for her with them. They did not treat my mother as a human. They fed her once a day, giving only sweet potatoes even though she was pregnant. She never got chapatis or nan bread. There was so much pain and tears, and she was always hungry. When my mother gave birth to me, she wanted to go back to my grandmother. But the problem was she didn't have the money for the train fare, so holding out her baby, she sat in the footpath begging for money. She had no luck after one day so she decided the only thing she could do was to give away the baby.

Then a very nice lady stopped to talk with her. Mom stood up and handed me to her and ran off. The lady took me to her home, and she and her husband became my loving parents, and they took good care of me as though I was their own. It was amazing how after a time, my mum's mental health improved until she became quite normal. They educated me through high school and then on to tertiary studies in computer science. I was about to graduate when I was hospitalised due to an ulcer. During my high school days, I loved to chew bubble gum which is not good to eat and eat sour mango sauce with too much vinegar. I would skip a meal because we did not have money to buy food in school because my father lost his job, and they had no income. So I stopped my vocational course. I became quite ill and suffered almost a year, always lying in bed. I didn't want to eat and or even take water as it's taste was bad, and I felt cold.

Then my adopted mother became ill with ovarian cancer and died. She had to give up being the nanny to a neighbours' child, and we did not have the money for her treatment. After her death, my adopted father brought another woman into the house. I didn't like her but couldn't say anything to dad. I felt so desperate at that time because I loved my new mom.

It was a crazy mixed-up family because my mom had 4 siblings, all with different fathers. Mom went to a village far away where she met some Muslim men, and five of them raped her.

Mom was pregnant again, so she had to do something to her tummy because she was always pregnant by different guys, and one of them was her maniac step-father. He ended up in jail and died in 2012 from goitre poisoning.

She has completely recovered and lives with her new family in a village in the mountain area of Orissa. She has found a guy who accepts her situation, and they live happily with their children. It was a sad story and the lady had kept it bottled up for so long that at last she felt she had to tell someone and decided that I would be the best one. Her two office friends were weeping, exclaiming, 'We had no idea of your terrible experiences.'

I visited a school operated by the Prakash family that had a great fondness for Ford vehicles. The school was sponsored by Compassion International. They took me from the railway station to their home in a beautifully restored 1947 Ford V8. The family also had a Ford A and a 1912 Model T, both in working order. They also had a very rare Ford Model T tractor of 1915 that was under repair. The Prakash family run a school of 440 children with only 5 teachers – that's 88 to class! They have a Sunday School of 244 children with only one teacher.

I visited several of the cities in this area. When I was at Khajuraho my hostess Miss Freer, suggested I visit the local temple as it was very famous and the only one of its kind in India. 'Would you like to be my guide?' I asked. She responded with a girlish giggle and suggested I just take a rickshaw as he'd know where to take me. I had no idea that this was a Hindu temple that tried to display the love the gods have for humans. There were many carvings and statures of men and women making love – no wonder the single lady was too embarrassed to guide me! As the writer Lawrence James states in his book Raj, 'All travellers to India were alternatively fascinated and repelled by the connection between religious practices and sexual enjoyment.'[10]

I was booked into the Harsh hotel which considers itself to be one of the oldest hotels in India. It was showing it's 100-plus year old history needing a complete refurbishment. My standard room was immense, easily three times the usual size of a double room. The bathroom was outsized to say the least, about the same size as

---

10 Lawrence James, *Raj*, Little, Brown and Company.

our lounge at home. All the plumbing worked but many years of polishing had worn the piping down to its original copper colour. It had a personal bearer service and my elderly gent couldn't do enough for me. Five minutes after bringing me my bed-tea, he was back again suggesting that surely I would like another cup. On checking in he carried my suitcase to the room. I had no sooner unlocked it than he opened it, spotted the dirty clothes and whisked them away to the laundry. He was back in five minutes beaming, 'Your clothes will be ready tonight sir.' He started work there on leaving school and was now in his 60th year.

But a recent complete refurbishment has changed it dramatically as a recent advertisement describes as follows:

> Hotel Harsh Ananda is a 'piece of history' in a unique & modern avatar. Furnished tastefully and equipped with all the modern state-of-the-art amenities to give you all the comfort you have always deserved . From the outside it retains its old world colonial charm, with a Victorian facade and lush green gardens on all sides.

About 60 kilometres from Allahabad is an annual mela or festival that is the world's largest donkey market at a place with the musical name of Sheetla Devi Dham, in the town of Kaushambi. A colleague said, 'This sir, is something that you must see. It is incomprehensible that so many donkeys can get bought and sold in one week. There will be 10,000 there. When you look you will see nothing but donkeys, donkeys and donkeys. Its funny how they treat the animals before the mela. They give them sweets and green grass so as to put them in a good mood.' Traders come from all over north India and even from Afghanistan.

The donkeys come in all colours from black to white and every conceivable shade of brown. Many are decorated by painting a white donkey's ears red and along the spine and the tip of the tail. Others have red spots painted all over them. This city has special significance to Hindus being the birthplace of one of their gods and the belief is that marriages contracted here will last.

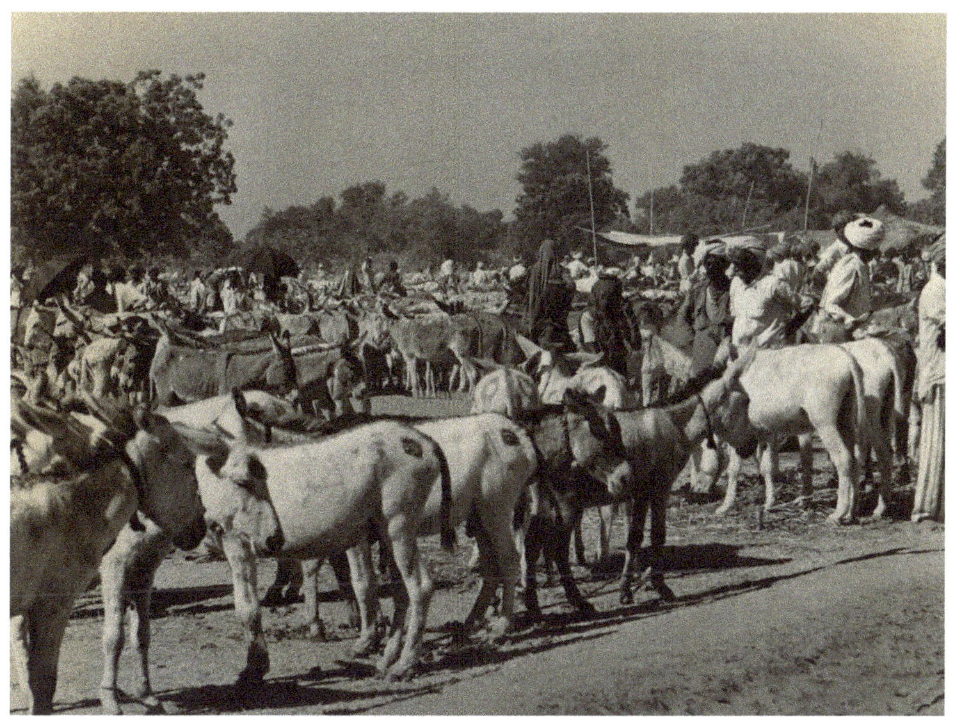

The largest donkey market in the world.

My colleague introduced me to a young man now in his employ, Pradham.

When Pradham became a Christian, his family received the news with great sadness and disappointment because they believed that as a Christian he would never grow up and be successful in his life. Pradham had been given a Nepali New Testament, and it fascinated him so much to have a book in his own language that he began to read it carefully.

"I began reading at the beginning of the book in the one called *Matthew.* I immediately sensed with my whole heart that this book was true. In fact everything in this book would be true. Now I realise that it was the Spirit of God convicting me, and I just accepted it. I decided that I must become a Christian and believe in Jesus Christ as my Saviour. But when I told my family about my new found faith they could accept what I had done.

Pradham explained that his mother suffered from heart disease for many years, had become painfully ill, and was unable to sleep for more than three hours a night. But although she heard her son speak about Jesus Christ for five years she refused to become a Christian herself. The one day, she said to herself, "Enough is enough; I am going to follow the lord."

That night she was transformed," said Pradham, "She went to sleep at nine o'clock and slept right through until six next morning. I was not at home at the time, but as soon as I retuned, I saw how radiant my mother looked and knew in my heart that she had accepted Jesus Christ as her Lord and Saviour.

"When I asked her what had happened she replied, "It is not because I have been eating good food, it is the Lord who has changed me. The day I accepted Christ my whole physical being changed.

'The scriptures have changed our lives so radically and I am grateful to the Bible Society for making them available in my own language.'

'You had better come and meet my friend who has a great story to tell.' Raju had a good job in the railways signal factory. One of his workmates was a Christian and Raju considered him to be a very nice man. He was always kind and cheerful. One day he asked him if he could get him a Christian holy book. I asked him many times and he always refused me making excuses that he couldn't get one. Finally he found a shop selling them and he began to read it very carefully. It took him many weeks to read it right through. He was sure it was the truth and decided to believe in Jesus and become a Christian.

He knew that his Muslim parents would not be pleased. They were so angry they drove him from the house telling him they would rather see him dead than come back to them. A couple of his Muslim workmates ganged up on him and blamed him for an engineering mistake that had nothing to do with him. He was sacked. Above all, his wife turned her back on him and demanded a divorce. 'Now I have no wife, no family, no job but I have salvation in Christ. And none of those have got it.'

But India is changing. During the time I worked there Christians for the most part were free to evangelise among the Hindus and Muslims. But more and more states are legislating against Hindus converting to Christianity.

The percentage of Christians has increased substantially from 2.5% a decade ago to about 5.8% today. That represents a huge increase in the growth rate.

Missiologist and church growth expert C. Peter Wagner has been receiving reports that the percentage may actually be 25% Christian — at least in parts of this large country — most of the growth coming in the past 10 to 15 years. And the growth may not all be in traditional churches. A substantial part may come from Jesus-follower groups within the Hindu culture. It is not uncommon for some Hindus, on learning about Jesus Christ, have adopted him to join their plethora of gods. They can see that he is a good man, a remarkable healer and a great teacher. But there has been periods when Christians were attacked by Hindus. "Four more churches in eastern India have been burnt after a week of religious violence that has driven thousands of people from their homes and into hiding. At least 14 people have died in attacks by groups of Hindus, who went on the rampage after a Hindu leader was killed last week. Reports say more than 60 churches in the state of Orissa have been burnt and around 3,000 homes have been destroyed as mobs tore through mainly Christian villages. *The Guardian* Mon 1 Sep 2008 11.46 BST

KUMBH MELA

On one visit my colleague Ron Penny suggested that it was time to prepare for a special outreach at Hindu's largest festival known as the Kumbh Mela. This is held every 12 years at the confluence of India's holy rivers, the Ganges and the Yamuna. Pilgrims come to bathe at this holy place in the belief that their sins will be washed away. One of my responsibilities as the distribution consultant to the Bible Society of India was to encourage the staff to discover every possible way to get the Bible into the hands of the people. Churches needed all the help they could get to do this. There were two major uses for the Scriptures: the provision of the complete Bible for Christians and to provide them with smaller editions that could be used in evangelism. These were called Portions and Selections of Scripture.

A team of a dozen young people assembled at Sonpur. There was no way we could get local accommodation so we took our own tents. They were set up in a vacant space near the railway yards. A couple of guys dug a toilet erecting a simple shelter around it. Our cook used an open fire and produced some remarkably good food. He only had two saucepans - one for rice and the other for meat and vegetables. He couldn't make chapatis. There was no water so we sent Antony Harrop off to see what he could get. This was in the days before bottled water that nowadays is available everywhere in the world. He came back with a case of Limca. This is a sweet lime cordial. It quenched the thirst ok but all that sugar caused us all put on weight.

The great melas of India were wonderful opportunities to contact large numbers of people in a short time. When I learned about the Sonpur Mela I encouraged the staff to make a special effort to reach as many people as possible by providing free Selections of Scripture.

The Mela was known as a huge animal market and is described in *Wikipedia* as follows:

> 'Many farm animals can be bought at the Sonpur mela from all breeds of dogs, buffaloes, donkeys, ponies, Persian horses, rabbits, goats and even the occasional camel. Many varieties of birds and poultry are also available. The area that attracts all, however, is the Haathi Bazaar where elephants are lined up for sale. The Sonpur Fair is the only place where such a large number of elephants are traded — although nowadays they cannot legally be sold. Numerous stalls are also set up at the grounds of the Sonpur Cattle Fair. A major attraction is the sight of numerous elephants, beautifully decorated for the purpose of sale. Trade in elephants has been prohibited at Sonpur Mela since 2004 owing to strict enforcement of Wildlife Protection Act, 1972 and further denial of transfer of ownership certificate to the elephant owners. '[11]

At the time we were there, about 90,000 elephants were on sale when the new laws forbidding their sale were still being ignored. It was a great experience to walk about the fair with great elephants on all sides. But things began to change when the law was enforced. In 2001, the number of elephants brought to Sonpur Mela was 354, while in 2016, only 13 elephants made it to the fair, but only for display, not for sale. In 2017, there were 3 tuskers at the fair.

11 Wikipedia.

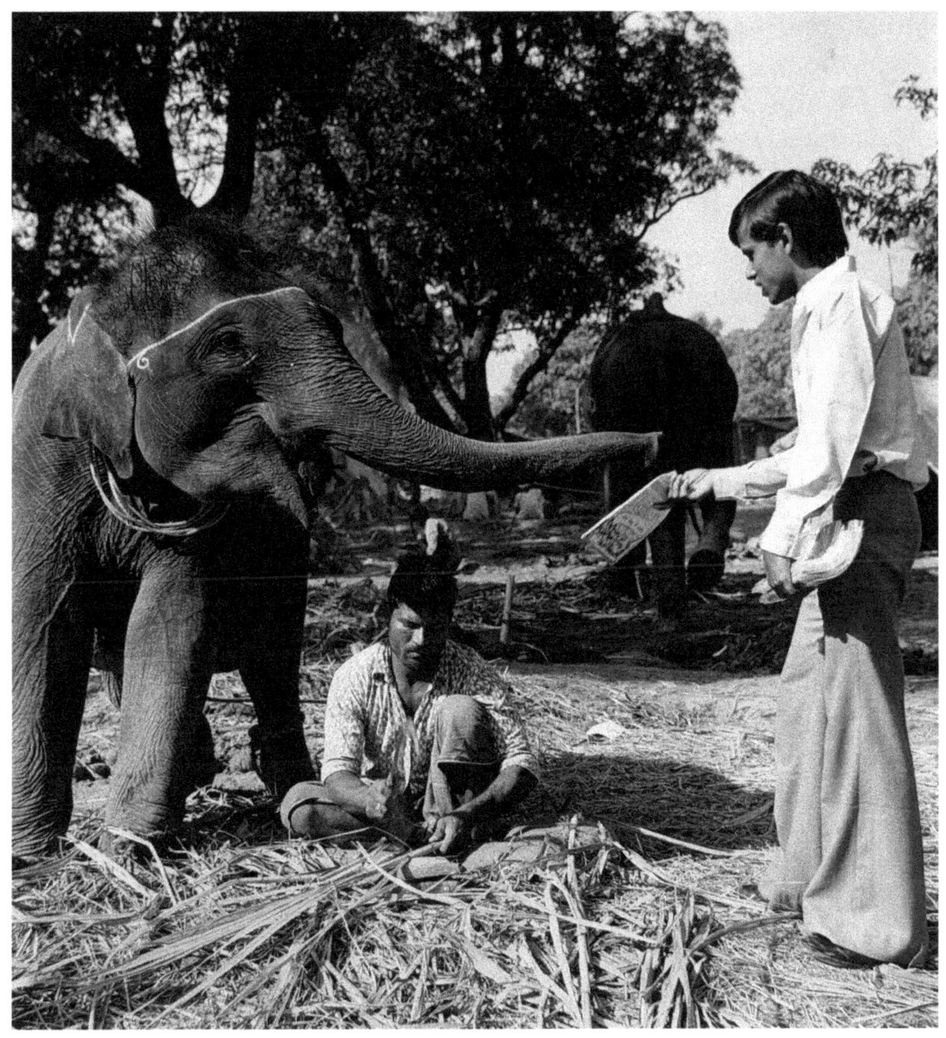

Literate (!) elephant, Sonpur Mela.

Knowing that an elephant eats enormous quantities of food and water I asked people where they get all the food needed for such a vast number of these creatures. They can eat from 200-600 pounds of food and up to 50 gallons -190 litres of water every day. Trainloads of fodder came every day.

The local railway station is an important junction and is connected to all parts of India. At the time of the Mela, trains bring hundreds of thousands of pilgrims and traders. The main platform is one of the longest railway platforms in the world – 2,415 ft (736 m.) – capable of accommodating a train of 32 carriages.

This is an important Hindu centre and ceremonial bathing in

the Ganges is held by Hindus to be unusually efficacious. On the day of the full moon an immense crowd assembles to bathe in the sacred water. Hindus believe that taking a dip in the sacred river will cleanse them of sins, purify their soul and liberate them from the cycle of birth and death – as the ultimate goal of Hinduism is salvation.

But, back to the Kumbh mela. It truly is a remarkable spectacle when literally millions of pilgrims come from all over India. It seems impossible to count them because the official estimates, such as for 2019, it was given as 'approximately 30 to 50 million.' Indian railways declared that they were anticipating 100,000,000 passengers for the event. One newspaper reported that Indian Railways will run 800 special trains during the festival some from away as 1,600 km. It is the largest gathering of human beings for a single religious purpose on the planet. It lasts for about three months. About 30,000 police are on hand to keep order. Huge tent cities are set up and many people just sleep in the open air. The problems of sanitation are best not described here. There are a about a thousand ashrams and hotels providing accommodation and several hospitals are setup.

I'm writing this in 2025 and for the mela this year the Indian Railways will operate 13,000 trains, including 10,000 regular and 3,000 special trains, over 50 days, including 2-3 additional days before and after the event.

The Hindi Times gives a few astounding statistics the authorities dealt with viz:-

- 160,000 tents
- 40,000 police and security officials
- 15,000 sanitation workers
- 67,000 street lights
- 150,000 toilets

Teams of young men moved among the traders and pilgrims offering free Christian Scriptures. It was always astonishing to me that they were always accepted and that there were practically none thrown away. About one million were given out every day and I saw only two that had been discarded. That is, only two found on the ground. The fact is that many Hindus also revere Christ Jesus placing him in a position of one of the gods whom they need to worship on the altar in their homes. I listened to one young man explain to a Hindu pilgrim that the god of this book , the Christians' book, the Bible, is the only one who offers the forgiveness of sins and true peace with God, right now, as soon as we confess our sins to him and turn away from them.

'Umm,' said the man, 'This is something I truly must look into because I'm wanting those things. I've been giving, working, searching and bathing all my life for it.'

They come to learn more about their faith and hear holy men, called *sadhus,* give their teachings. There are usually about a thousand of them, who form the central attraction. Each of them has a way of demonstrating their beliefs. They range from terrible starvation to gorging on one type of food. From burying their head in the ground to stretching the penis by rolling it on a stick. Another might not stop talking until he falls asleep, or his followers force him to eat something. One ascetic I saw has had his right arm raised for seven years. Another has been standing for eight months and aims to do so for another 43 months. Most of them never seem to wash or bathe, cut their hair or wear any clothes. It seems that the more extreme the more holy they are! But in general, the people respect them for the efforts they make to be different.

When I asked a couple of pilgrims what they thought of them they said that it is because they try so hard to please their gods that we respect them. One man we talked to said, "The reason I take a bath in these sacred waters is to achieve immortality ... immortality of the soul. It felt amazing, it always feels amazing... Normally only the body gets wet but here you actually feel like your inner self is getting wet, your heart, your soul is getting wet, your spirit... The depth of my being is being touched." One woman, whom I could see was quite a refined lady and was happy to chat with me. She was a bank manager. She told me that she had bathed every day for a week. "I can feel that my sins are gradually being washed away and that's because I have a special way of bathing. I wear only a sari, nothing else, so that the water washes all my skin. I make sure that my breasts are uncovered when I go down into the water. If a sadhu sees them he will cleanse me from sin. If possible, I ask him to touch me there, because that makes the sin go faster."

So I asked her if, deep in her heart, she feels her sins are cleared away and forgiven and that she has the peace of God in her heart. 'Oh no,' she said, 'It's not possible to know these things.' I introduced her to a lady member of our team who I hoped could help her find the way of salvation as offered by the Lord Jesus Christ. I quoted the words of the Gospel: "If we confess our sins, he is faithful and just to forgive us our sins, and cleanse us from all unrighteousness.

'Really,' she said, 'Is that from your holy book?'

"Let me introduce you to my friend Sunita over there, she has some literature you might like to see. She has got a leaflet entitled *Who can Free us From Sin and Death?* I'm sure it can help you."

Taking it reverently in her hands, she glanced at it and said, "You had better give me a few copies for my friends and family. They all need it."

'Sure,' we said, 'We printed a million copies. What is your language? We have it in Hindi, Gujarati, Marathi, Tamil, Telegu, Bengali, Nepali, Urdu, Punjabi, Malayali and of course, English."

'Goodness, you are trying to reach everyone! Please give me Gujarati and English.'

'God loved the world,' said Sunita, 'and that includes all of us.'

Several hours later Sunita looked up from the food she was making, because she had felt sorry for the cook who was trying to make a meal for twelve people with only two pots, to see this same lady standing nearby. She said, 'I've come back to tell you that this has been such a wonderful experience. First of all I have my sins washed away in the holy water and I feel clean, and now also I've been forgiven by Jesus. I'm following him from now on.

In addition to the thousands of naked ones there are thousands of brightly coloured Sadhus many of whom are teachers of the faith. They are clad in clothes of red, yellow, orange and saffron and some are quite spectacular. Sadhus range from the naked ones who don't wear anything all year round to some dressed in the finest silk. Some claim to have no earthly possessions and have no pockets to fill and others who are exceedingly rich. Recently I heard of a company that makes a special cover for cell phones with a strap so that a holy man with no pockets can hang it around his neck!

These men have a special place in Indian society. They are deeply revered and looked up to for guidance and blessings. Yet, having neither means of income, nor a place to stay. They live as beggars owning nothing and depend entirely on donations of strangers.

CHAPTER SIXTEEN

ASIATIC LIONS AND BENGAL TIGERS

Not far from Bangalore is an animal reserve in which are two species that I wanted to observe. It is home to Bengal tigers (*Panthera tigris tigris)* and the rare Asiatic lion (*Panthera leo persica.*) I took a bus tour in an old bus that was only just holding together. It rattled and banged in such a way that I envisioned it scaring away any animals. But incredibly, I was fortunate to see both these famous felines. After an hour or so the bus stopped at a quite thickly wooded place and then a few minutes later, three tigers appeared. They came up very close to the bus and sniffed around it, luckily coming to my side of the bus. These are the second largest of the cat family. The Siberian tiger is about 600-750 lb (272.1-340.2 kg) with a body length of 10-12 ft (3-3.7 m), with some males weighing 900 lb (408.2 kg) or more. The Bengal is a little smaller, but truly majestic all the same.

Then suddenly the guide pointed to the other side of the bus and said, 'Look there. The lions!'

Sure enough in the forest shade were two Asiatic lions. One stood out fairly clearly then moved in to deeper shade. The beside him another appeared. The guide was beside himself with excitement. Later he said that we were extremely lucky to have seen them and declared that he had not seen them for many months. It was quite dark in the deep shade, so I had to use maximum exposure and the slowest shutter speed without a tripod. I asked the driver to turn off the engine and for everyone to be perfectly still so that there would be no vibration. The result was satisfactory with a ghostly atmosphere. A game reserve in Gujarat states that all the Asiatic lions in the country are in their reserve and a couple of Guidebooks agree. But my guide in Karnataka disputes that. 'You've seen them yourself. We have them too.' He said, 'but the fact is we don't talk about ours so as to protect them. All the other game parks are so jealous of us.'

KASHMIR

One day in 1980 I flew on a British Airways 747 from Hong Kong to Delhi. We left at 9 pm giving me time to attend one of our office girl's wedding, Helen Wu. It was completely full. I was booked in at the Shilton Hotel that seemed to be trying to pretend it was part of the Hilton empire. It was winter and there was only one blanket available. They refused me another, so I took down the curtains and used them as extra blankets. It was 4C. Then on to Srinagar, Kashmir where there was snow on the ground. I booked into, not a hotel as requested, but a houseboat named *Helal* and owned by Sultan Wagnu. It was moored on the beautiful blue Dal lake and measured about 51x18 feet. The main cabin had a double bed. There was a spacious lounge, bathroom, kitchen, wood stove and heater. It was like camping in luxury. The houseboy Ali was very attentive and was at my beck and call, tempting me with food and drinks.

The flight was delayed by several hours, but this didn't deter my host from giving me a warm welcome. He was Sultan Wagnu, the owner of the houseboat hotel. In later years, this group owned many boats. My travel agent had suggested I stay in a houseboat, but I insisted on being booked into a hotel. Its name fooled us both.

My guide, knowing that I was a Christian, was very anxious to show me the tomb of Christ.

There is a belief that Jesus survived the crucifixion and spent his remaining years in Kashmir. He didn't go to England that the English like to sing about in the poem by William Blake: *"And did those feet in ancient time, walk upon England's mountains green? And was the holy Lamb of God on England's pleasant pastures seen?"* But some say he imbibed the teachings of the Buddha who lived about 500 years before Christ. There is a disreputable building with a three-tier roof on the corner of a back street in Srinagar called the Rozabal Shrine. The watchman showed me a large sarcophagus covered with a green cloth.

It was becoming increasingly popular with New Age Christians, unorthodox Muslims and fans of the Da Vinci Code. My guide insisted it was a mosque but I think he was mixing up the original use of this building in that it was the tomb of Youza Asaph, a medieval Muslim preacher.

There are two tombs inside the Roza Bal, one tomb is of Ziarati Hazrati Youza Asouph or Yuz Asaph (or Asaf) who died in 112

AD., and another grave is of Syed Nasir-u-Din (Islamic saint, a descendant of Imam Moosa Ali Raza, said to be a great devotee of Jesus, who buried here in 1451).

The Hebrew name of Jesus was Yuza, in Arabic or in the Koran his name was Hazrat Isa or Isa. Farhang-Asafia, which explains how Jesus healed a leper and then became Asaf (purified or healed) and the word Yuz mean "Leader". Yuz Asaph or Youza Asouph means "Leader of the Healed" which pointed to Jesus Christ. The grave of Yuz Asaph also points east to west, according to Jewish tradition but the Muslim tombs are always points on the north-south axis.

Photography is strictly prohibited and the shrine is now closed permanently.[12] Despite this prohibition, I was permitted to take one shot.

We borrowed a jeep from the Church of North India and went to Korkernag and Pelegan that are about at about 7,000 ft asl. It was all day round trip. The beautiful countryside was enveloped with snow. The people live in one or three storied houses of stone and wood. There were many apple orchards. I believe it was the famous apples of Kashmir that helped to make the place famous since its founding in 6 BC.

I noticed that many men and women appeared to have huge bellies and I asked someone what caused them to look so fat. He laughed and explained that under the coat was a small basket of hot coals. This kept the person warm. So I joked and said, 'So you can't tell if a woman is pregnant or fat.' He laughed loudly and called a man over to show me his 'heater.' It was made of a closely woven basket enclosing a small pot of burning coals called a *kangri*.

Outwardly everything was quite peaceful but my guide was very careful in his dealing with the public subtilty shielding me from have conversations with people he did not know. Someone asked him if I had spent a lot of time in India, suggesting by his question that I wasn't in India now, Kashmir is closely related to Pakistan. As soon as we were clear of him my guide explained that the feelings were still raw with India. 'So many people here have died because of India,' I was told. I checked that later found that at least 30,000 have been killed in fierce skirmishes between Indian and Pakistan supporters. The state of Jammu and Kashmir was still a hot bed and suffering from the loss of tourists, both foreign and domestic.

12 Creative Commons Attribution-Share Alike 4.0 International.

It appeared to me to be a three-way fight. India wants Kashmir. Pakistan claims it. And a bunch of locals want independence from them both. When my boss heard that I had been there he was not pleased thinking that it was too dangerous. .

I was keen to meet the translators of the Bible into Kashmiri but my guide felt that it was unwise as it could bring trouble to them. Officially I was to preach at the Anglican Church on the Sunday so it was arranged that I could meet them there.

On the Sunday I spoke at the rebuilt All Saints Church. A group of Muslims had tried to burn it down last year. It was -4C so I kept on all my warm clothing while I preached. The minister posted special security men around the church fearing repercussions from militant Muslims who might object to a foreigner preaching. He alerted the police and the army and they sent plain clothed officers to form a tight ring around the church.

The main translator Predhuman K Joseph Dhar had begun the work in 1994. He was assisted by Father Jim Borts, a Mill Hill missionary who has been in Kashmir since 1963. Dhar, a noted scholar, journalist, writer and educator, became a convert to Catholicism after many years of searching for inner peace that he did not find in Islam.

He studied in the mission school in Mill Hill. He secretly visited the church fearing that his parents would find out. An Italian nun, Sister Priscilla helped him to understand the gospel. Predhuman was baptized April 21, 1984. He was examined by a group of his father's Hindu friends, members of a very old and conservative Shavite Brahminical order. The result was that both his father and mother officially disinherited him. He was thrown out of the house and was abandoned by his siblings and the whole clan. Only his wife and three children loyally stayed by his side. He steadfastly continued to translate and was rewarded to see the Kashmiri Bible published in 2011 but launched in a ceremony in Andra Pradesh, well away from the disputed region.

It was a great pleasure to meet the Rev Jonathan the local Church of North India pastor and S.S. Gerben, the grandson of the Tibetan Bible translator. When Bishop Chandu Ray stayed in our home in Fiji during the Bible Week in 1969, he told me the remarkable story of the translation of the Tibetan Bible. It's such a great story I reproduce it here courtesy of the Bible Society.

The story of the Tibetan Bible may be summarised as follows:

Dr A. W. Heyde and Mr Pagel, members of the Moravian church, felt called to preach the Gospel in the closed land of Tibet. Their first attempt to enter the forbidden land was from western China and ended when they were set upon by bandits and robbed. They then travelled to India and climbed the Himalayas to Darjeeling, but this time they were turned back by Tibetan border guards.

Over the next year or so they made repeated efforts to enter Tibet, constantly moving westwards, until in 1858 they came to the Luba Valley near Leh. There they found a small Tibetan settlement that had grown up around the home of a Tibetan nobleman called Tempu Gergan.

Tempu had been Minister of Finance during the minority of the Dalai Lama and when, a few months after taking power in 1855, the young Dalai Lama was found dead, it was suspected that officials of the regency were responsible for giving him poison. Tempu had fallen out with the State Oracle and when the Oracle accused him in full seance of being the guilty man, Tempu was not surprised. He had made his preparations and was ready. Much of his wealth had already been sent secretly out of Lhasa and he was able to slip out of the building and escape just in time.

The journey from Lhasa mountains to the Luba Valley was an arduous one, but once outside Tibetan jurisdiction, Tempu and his household settled down. Three years later they welcomed the two strangers and when Tempu saw how disappointed they were at being unable to enter his homeland, he invited them to live with him, promising to teach them the Tibetan language and help them translate their holy book in exchange for their medical skills.

Unfortunately, although the two men quickly became proficient in spoken Tibetan, the task of translating the Bible was more difficult than they had imagined. In the first place there was the problem of which dialect of Tibetan they should use: Tempu and his family spoke the Lhasa dialect, but it was not well understood by people in either east or west of the country. Amdo Tibetan, which was the eastern dialect, was regarded as barbaric by the people of Lhasa and was even less understood by those in the west.

The solution appeared to be to use Classical Tibetan as found in the Kanjur, the holy book of Tibetan Buddhism. However there were still problems, for the words of the Kanjur frequently had meanings that were opposed to Christian ideas. For example, the word for "god" referred both to divine beings and also to the living buddhas such as the Dalai Lama. By using this word, the Biblical statement "Jesus is God" becomes nothing more than an affirmation that Jesus is on the same level as any other reincarnation. It was the same with the word for "prayer", which in Tibetan included not only the endless chanting of the phrase "Om mani padme hum", but also the fluttering of prayer flags or the turning of the ubiquitous prayer wheels.

In addition, Classical Tibetan was rapidly becoming obsolete and would be as difficult for the ordinary Tibetan to understand as Shakespearian English is for the modern-day Englishman.

In 1885 Tempu's wife Droma gave birth to a son, to whom was given the name Sonam. As the boy grew older he enjoyed listening to the Bible stories told by the two missionaries and became interested in their religion, possibly as a result of hearing his father discuss the Bible with them as they wrestled with the problems of translation.

When Tempu died in 1897, followed a short time later by his wife, the twelve-year old Sonam openly declared his intention of becoming a Christian and was baptised, taking the Christian name of Yoseb (Joseph). He asked his missionary friends to send him to school where he could learn Christian doctrine and Western science. In his absence Hyde, Pagel and an expert in Oriental languages, Dr Jaeschke, continued to struggle with the translation. They made slight progress, for about this time they finished the Gospel of John and had it printed at Kyelang in Kashmir.

When Tempu died Heyde and Pagel felt that there was nothing further to keep them in the Luba Valley and moved to Leh, where they established a small Tibetan church. Despite this success, however, they were greatly discouraged by the fact that their translation of John was not well received. People in the east could hardly understand the language and the translation was stilted and difficult to read.

When Yoseb Gergan finished his education at the age of 21 he turned down the offer of a good position with the British government and returned home, intending to settle down on the estate he had inherited. Heyde and Pagel asked him to come to Leh to serve as pastor of the Tibetan church and for some time Yoseb was uncertain what he should do, but as the result of a dream he decided to accept the call. He divided his estate among his servants and retainers and moved to Leh.

There he found that Dr Jaeschke had died and been replaced by another Oriental scholar, Dr Francke, who was continuing to work on translating the Bible, but though his efforts were better, they were still not good enough. Yoseb, as well as his pastoral duties, worked with Dr Francke, but progress was very slow and unsatisfactory.

One day Yoseb encountered an old monk in an isolated temple and overheard him chanting from an ancient book of myths and legends. The dialect was one that appeared to pre-date both Classical Tibetan and the various contemporary dialects. Although nearly forgotten, it was familiar enough to be understood by all and, even better, it had words for "god" and "prayer" and other concepts that were free of the Buddhist connotations associated with the more familiar words.

Yoseb asked to be allowed to borrow the book so that he could study its language, but the lama graciously gave it to him, pleased that it would continue to be valued after his own death. Using this ancient language as their key, Francke and Yoseb worked more quickly on a new translation of the Bible, a work Yoseb continued on his own after Francke returned to Europe. In 1935, after twenty-three years of effort, Yoseb finished the task. All that remained was to have the book printed.

When he contacted the Bible Society, however, he discovered a problem. There was no Tibetan typeface. Like the Urdu and Arabic Bibles, the entire document had to be written by hand in a clear and consistent script, and then either engraved or reproduced photographically. There was no facility in India to undertake such a massive project, so with great trepidation Yoseb sent his precious manuscript to the British and Foreign Bible Society (B&FBS) in London.

Before committing expensive resources to the project, the B&FBS wanted to have it checked and submitted it to Oriental scholars. In the days before photocopiers, it was laborious and time-consuming to make copies of Yoseb's manuscript, but this was done and as well as experts from the universities in Britain, the B&FBS sent copies to China and India where it was assessed by missionaries and scholars on the borders of Tibet.

The result was positive. "Never would we have believed a Tibetan text would be so readily accepted by the diverse Tibetan peoples," was the report. However a number of questions were raised which needed to be answered, but before Yoseb could be consulted World War II broke out and work had to be suspended.

During the war the precious Tibetan manuscript was sent to Rippon in Yorkshire for safe-keeping and one night a 2,000 lb bomb landed outside the cathedral crypt, just four feet away from the Tibetan Bible. The bomb disposal squad could find no fault to explain why the bomb had not exploded and the sexton was convinced that God had protected the ancient cathedral and its contents.

By the time the war ended the B&FBS was struggling to rebuild and to carry out other projects that seemed more urgent. Prompted by Yoseb Gergan, who was now 60, the Indian Bible Society (IBS) requested that the manuscript be returned to them, as technological developments meant that they were now able to handle such work.

They were dismayed to find, however, that Yoseb had used cheap Tibetan paper which had suffered badly from the effects of time and damp. The paper had yellowed and it was impossible to obtain a clear picture of the writing. The only solution was to re-write the whole thing on special white paper – but in the aftermath of the war, such paper was in short supply and eventually the staff of the IBS produced their own paper by taking ordinary paper and coating it with a special mixture of chemicals and egg-white.

The manuscript and the special paper was sent back to Yoseb in Leh so that he could re-write it and at the same time make a few necessary corrections. After two years of labour, however, Yoseb suffered a stroke. Miraculously he recovered but he was too weak to continue writing and so two scribes – Gappel and Phunthsog – did the writing at his dictation. After a while they were supplemented by another two – Stobldan and Zodpa – with the result that it is possible to detect five different handwritings in the finished book. (The same applies to the Urdu Bible, where some pages are written in a fine, bold hand and others in a small, cramped hand. One of the minor prophets is particularly hard to read!)

On August 11, 1946, the work was finally finished and five days later Yoseb Gergan, one of the great saints of God, died.

The completed manuscript was sent to Lahore for printing, but the process of preparing the proofs revealed a number of problems, particularly in the final part of the book where pages had been corrected instead of re-written. Chandu Ray, secretary of the IBS, decided to send the proofs back to Leh so that one of the Tibetan scribes could correct them. This involved a 50-day journey by a courier (with another 50 days for the return trip) and a Tibetan called Sandrup set off, promising to return in four months' time.

He never arrived (his body was found the following year where he had been overwhelmed by an avalanche) and after a long delay another set of proofs was prepared and second courier, a Christian called Bahadur, set off for Leh. As he crossed the final pass, however, a ferocious storm struck him, leaving him unconscious and deaf from the lightning and thunder that struck all around him. When he recovered he staggered into Leh only to find that water had been driven into the saddlebags and the proofs were nothing more than a mass of sodden paper.

A third set of proofs were sent, accompanied by intense prayer. Despite the rioting and fighting that had broken out as India and Pakistan separated, this parcel was entrusted to the regular postal service and to everyone's relief arrived safely. As he studied the proofs, Gappel found so many minor errors – for example, where the process of reproduction had missed out a thinner or fainter than usual tail to a letter, thus turning it into another sound entirely – that Gappel decided he would have to go to Lahore and correct the actual printing plates. Despite considerable opposition from his family, Gappel set out on horseback to travel through the mountains to Lahore.

Months passed and no word was heard of Gappel until a beggar came to the IBS office with a cryptic note that quoted the last verse of the Bible: "Come ... quickly come." When questioned the beggar revealed that it had been given to him by an old man who was living in a small hut, trapped between the Indian and Pakistani armies and in constant danger from both. As an obvious foreigner (Tibetans, like Chinese, have slanting eyes and stubby noses whereas hill-country Indians tend to have large hooked noses and wide eyes) he dared not venture out, but had entrusted his message to the beggar.

Chandu Ray asked the new Pakistan government for help, but

with the fighting that was going on all along the border the officials declared that there was nothing they could do. Ray therefore decided that he would have to travel to Kashmir himself. He travelled by train to Amritsar – a perilous decision, as trains were regularly stopped by one side or the other and either all the Hindus or all the Muslims massacred. The fact that Ray was a Christian would, in the turmoil, be little protection.

There was a regular flight from Amritsar to Srinagar, but as Ray waited in the airport lounge with his ticket in his hand the government announced that all flights were cancelled. He immediately prayed and then spoke to the airport manager, pointing out that such a last-minute cancellation meant a lot of angry passengers who would, at the very least, demand a full refund of their tickets. The manager, who did not have that much money, quickly declared that the flight would proceed after all and the announcement would apply only to future flights.

Ray then made his way to the fighting line near where the beggar had told him Gappel was hiding. Presenting himself as an official of the IBS he obtained permission to distribute Christian books to the soldiers and gradually worked his way closer to the front. When evening came on he was very close to No-man's Land and accepted hospitality from a squad of soldiers. As they sat around the camp fire he handed out copies of the Gospels and explained the power of the Christian book. Seeing that his words received a ready reception from the bored soldiers, he told first of how the Bible had changed his own life and then told the story of the Tibetan Bible.

One of the Indian officers was sufficiently intrigued to offer to take Ray across the bridge into No-man's Land to look for the scribe, at the same time warned that failure to find him would result in a charge of spying with the inevitable death penalty. Chandu could tell he wasn't joking and committing himself to God set off. He was difficult to find as he had built a small shelter. Fortunately Gappel and the corrected proofs were still there and the surprised and relieved officer escorted them back to the Indian lines. As they parted, he remarked that Ray's name had made him suspect that Ray was from Pakistan and he had decided on taking him to search for the scribe in order to test whether he was an honest man or not.

Back in Srinagar, however, the government ban on civilian flights had come into effect. The road journey was difficult, dangerous and long, so Ray went to the government official in charge of issuing permits and told him the story of the Tibetan Bible. He was very angry that a Pakistani should approach him like that but he listened to Chandu tell the story of the Tibetan Bible and was amazed at what he heard. So his initial anger and suspicion at the presence of an enemy Pakistani gave way to amazement and the man gave him the required passes for the daily flight to Delhi.

Once in Delhi, however, a different problem arose. Gappel was used to the coolness of 10,000 foot mountains and the dry heat of the plains struck him like a blow. He quickly became feverish and it seemed likely that he would die! Ray and other Christians prayed to God for help and that afternoon the monsoon rains, normally as regular as clockwork, started several weeks early. Gappel revived sufficiently to catch the train to Lahore.

Lahore is slightly cooler than Delhi, but it was still too hot for poor Gappel, who grew increasingly distressed. By afternoon, when the air was still and even the crows drooped in the shade gasping for breath, Gappel was clearly heading for heatstroke. In desperation Ray contacted the ice factory and had a truck-load of ice delivered to the IBS office. The room where Gappel worked was lined with huge blocks of ice and with the fan stirring up a hurricane of freezing air the scribe set to work, beaming happily.

A sense of urgency possessed everyone at the press. As Gappel corrected each plate it was rushed away and fitted to the printing press. The manager and workers laboured for twelve hours a day to keep the pages pouring from the press and Gappel himself worked even longer hours, often as much as twenty hours a day. Ninety years after Heyde and Pagel first started to translate the word of God, the finished book was ready!

Gappel, stoutly refusing to risk his life in the "devil machines" of plane and train, bought a pony and set off for Leh with his saddlebags filled with Bibles. He was received with joy by friends and family who had long given him up for lost, and then entered the church to give thanks to God. For the very first time a Tibetan Bible was opened on the pulpit and the words of life were read to an eager and expectant congregation.

On this page from the Tibetan Bible, John 3:16 is underlined.

We may wonder why God permitted so many years to pass before His word was available in the language of Tibet. In part, no doubt, the delay was because the devil so actively opposed the work. It is no exaggeration to say that Tibet was the devil's kingdom, where his power was actively displayed. The fanatical opposition of monks and government meant that foreigners – including missionaries – were excluded from the country and printed literature sent in was either destroyed or ignored by an illiterate population.

Ten years after the Bible was printed, the Chinese communists, in an act of unprovoked aggression, invaded Tibet. Unlike the western "imperialists" they so loudly condemned, who might have invaded and controlled but who would have respected local religion and customs, the Chinese committed fearful atrocities, actively destroying monasteries and temples and massacring monks and nuns. Within a few short years the centuries-old power of Tibetan Buddhism was effectively ended and now the Christian gospel is being preached in Tibet by Chinese Christians and the Tibetan Bible is being read by a newly literate population.

One of my last jobs before resigning the first time from the Bible Society was to republish this Bible. This posed some difficulties because it was a hand-written script the book was quite large. So it was a major challenge for our production consultant Henk Dymn to reproduce it in a handy size but keeping the written scripts readable.

After Kashmir I flew to Delhi and had dinner with Captain Wardher, had a meeting with Ron Penny. Next morning Ron and I flew to Agra. We visited the Agra Fort then the Taj Mahal. The Fort is a massive structure built in 1565. It has 2.5km of massive walls 20 metres high and a ten metre moat. Our guide was anxious to show us the shish mahal or mirror palace which is said to be the haram dressing room. All the walls and ceiling are covered with small mirrors. One candle lit is reflected in all these mirrors for a startling effect. The glass was imported from Syria.

CHAPTER SEVENTEEN

A FAMOUS HOSPITAL

Vellore, in South India is the home of the Christian Medical College and Hospital. This is a very famous hospital founded by Dr Paul Brand. He is noted for his work of reconstructing the limbs of leprosy patients. Compassion Int., sponsored the children of the hospital staff as well as children of lepers living in their special village nearby. Leprosy, also known as Hansen's disease, is spread, not by touch, but in many cases by droplets containing the bacteria from the infected person's nose. It is interesting to note that under Jewish law as portrayed in the Bible, lepers had to cover their faces. That was clearly not to cover embarrassing disfigurements but prevent the spread of nasal drops.

At the time of writing the number of cases world-wide was about 216,000 but when I was at the hospital it was 5.2 million. Concerted effort by the World Health Organisation supporting governments and organisations like the Leprosy Mission has greatly reduced the number. Founded in 1874, The Leprosy Mission is the oldest and largest leprosy-focused organisation in the world today. In the twenty years from 1994 to 2014, 16 million people worldwide were cured of leprosy.13

My Compassion worker first took me to the village. The people lived in very simple houses, more like tidy clean shacks. The state of these places impressed me and my colleague said, 'These people know that cleanliness is next to godliness.' Their deformities and suffering did not deter them from trying to live tidy lives. Everyone greeted me warmly knowing that I represented their childrens' sponsors. The first person I met was a woman of about thirty. She came out of her house and quickly bent to touch my feet – the ultimate show of respect. I could see no deformities and when I asked her how she was, she rubbed her stomach. She was wearing only a sari and moved a fold and pushed it down as far as her black

13 Wikipedia.

pubic hair saying, 'Its here. Here.' Such an action in any society would have been quite unacceptable but in this case, it showed how she had lost all feelings of respect and modesty. My guide began to apologise explaining that all her life she has been subjected to abuse and scorn and never been shown the slightest respect even as a beautiful young woman.

At the next hut a man grinning from ear to ear put out his hand. It was lacking a couple of fingers and a joint of his thumb. I had been told that it was quite ok to touch a leper so I took his hand in greeting. It was cold and hard. After a lifetime of thinking that one should never touch a leper it was a strange feeling to do so. But the warmth of their greetings and pleasure that I had visited them in their own homes was reward enough. But I have to confess, I washed my hands and arms the first chance I had still not really believing that I was not contaminated.

Paul Wilson Brand, the pioneering missionary surgeon who wrote a series of books connecting the Christian faith and medicine, was born in 1914 to missionary parents in the mountains of south-western India, Brand attended London University, where he met his wife, surgeon Margaret Berry. The two surgeons returned to Vellore, India, to teach at the Christian Medical College and Hospital. While working as the school's first professor of orthopaedics and hand research, Brand pioneered surgical work with those suffering from Hansen's disease. He was the first surgeon to use reconstructive surgery to correct deformities caused by the disease in the hands and feet, and developed many other forms of prevention and healing from the disease.

Before Brand, it was widely believed that those suffering from Hansen's disease lost their fingers and feet because of rotting flesh. Instead, Brand discovered, such deformities were due to the loss of ability to feel pain. With treatment and care, he showed, victims of the disease could go indefinitely without such deformities. It is one of the oldest diseases known as there are records dating back 600 years before Christ.

There were many lepers in the Tamil-speaking area of India a number of whom had become Christians. The Bible Society of India produced a special edition of the Tamil New Testament for them printed on very thick paper. This enabled a person with few or no fingers to turn the pages. I wanted to see for myself how they managed this special book so I visited a leper village. When I asked why there were so few men in the village, one said, 'Oh they have gone to work.' What he meant was that they had gone into the city to beg on the streets. He had no difficulty in turning the pages with stubby hard finger-short hands.

We knew an American missionary in Jakarta who was diagnosed with leprosy yet to her knowledge had had no contact whatsoever with an infected person. It was supposed to be a closely guarded secret but one of their 'friends' told me about it.

Lorraine had an awkward experience. Friends took her to a Leprosy Mission Hospital near Jakarta. Her plan was to have a rest while I was away with the children but friends insisted she accompany them on a visit to the hospital. While there she collapsed. They put her into a bed and tells how it felt rather strange being in a bed usually occupied by leper patients

I visited a school where we sponsored three hundred children. The last annual medical check found 161 have TB. I helped distribute a tonic for all the children.

My role in India was the Distribution and Information Consultant to the Bible Society of India. Distribution was the marketing and Information in the sense of obtaining information about the work that could be shared with other members of the United Bible Societies. They would be asked to support the work subsidising it by as much as half a million dollars. But to some of the staff, my visit was an opportunity to discuss their problems with a visitor. These could range from a request to buy a transistor radio so that they could listen to the cricket to matrimonial matters.

CHAPTER EIGHTEEN

EARTHQUAKE IN GUJARAT

I was in India for the Indian Independence celebrations in 1993 when I had an emergency call from the Bombay office. There had been a terrible 7.7 earthquake in Gujarat State, and the Bible Society was sending a team to help with the rescue efforts. Early reports suggested that as many as 13,000 people had been killed and 167,000 injured. Hundreds of villages had been demolished, including 340,000 buildings. The devastation was terrible to behold. Many of the village homes were built of stones and rocks, some not even mortared into place, and so had crumbled to the ground. The official record that became available later said that about one million structures had been destroyed or damaged, including two hospitals and eight schools. The number of buildings utterly destroyed or needing repair amounted to over 929,000.

A week after the quake and we were still in the area from 27th to 29th October, 1993, and as we walked through villages that had been destroyed, I was struck by the fact that we could smell decomposing corpses. That meant that living people had been caught and after a few days had died where they were. In whole villages, we saw not one living person. Sometimes there were one or two survivors who had stories to tell of their miraculous escape from death. One man said, 'I have always cursed my bladder because it made me get up in the night. But today, I thank the gods for it because I was out of the house relieving myself when it happened.'

There was a surreal silence as we poked around the ruins looking for survivors. I had always found India a noisy place, whether in a city or village. There was always traffic noise or a radio disturbing the peace, but not here. Occasionally we would find a man or woman who had lost everything, searching for something useful like a scrap of clothing, some food, or a container with which to get some water. We were in a dozen villages including Killarni, Umarga, Holi, Osmanabad, Solapur, Kolhapur and Udgir. where we saw not a single living soul but just hectares of jumbled rock and stones that had once been homes.

It was very difficult to move around as we climbed over all that debris. I slipped and skinned my leg much to the consternation of my colleagues. 'Be careful, sir, that will get infected here.' But I always carried a couple of plasters in my camera bag.

We found only one living person caught in the rubble of a home. We were climbing over a pile of stones when I caught sight of a piece of red cloth. I stopped to look more carefully. There was a slight movement and I moved a rock aside. It was a young woman of about twenty almost completely covered with the rocks from her home. I called to my colleagues to help, and we carefully moved the rocks that covered her head and body until we found that her legs were crushed and securely caught. She was wearing only a sari, and this had been partly torn off exposing her chest and lower abdomen. Her left breast had a huge cut right across, almost cutting it half. It had been ripped by a large nail protruding from what looked like a door frame. It was still stuck in her chest. A most ghastly sight.

She was unconscious and had been lying trapped for six days and nights. There was no way to release her and I hoped we could find a rescue team to help. We looked about, but there were none in the area so we decided to go back to her and perhaps offer some water that we carried. It was quite incredible that she was still alive: it was a wonder that she had not bled to death. But the blood from her injuries had stopped flowing and congealed. Holding her head in my hand, I poured a little into her mouth. Her eyes fluttered, and she muttered what sounded like 'abb, abb'; trying to say thank you in Gujarati – આભાર – Aabhaar. She took another mouthful, sighed deeply, and breathed her last. My two colleagues and I stood quietly for a minute or two, deeply moved. Then they asked me to commit her to God. Before leaving, we covered her body with stones to prevent animal scavengers. It could be days before she could be removed

As we walked away, one fellow said, 'Did you get a good photo?'

'No,' I answered, 'I couldn't do that.'

Beyond the earthquake area we found a small 'café' selling food. All we could buy was one chapati each smeared with sauce. The police had ordered food rationing to one chapati per person. As we ate, one of the men said of that young woman we had found; 'I've never seen anything like that. It was like great beauty and horror all together.'

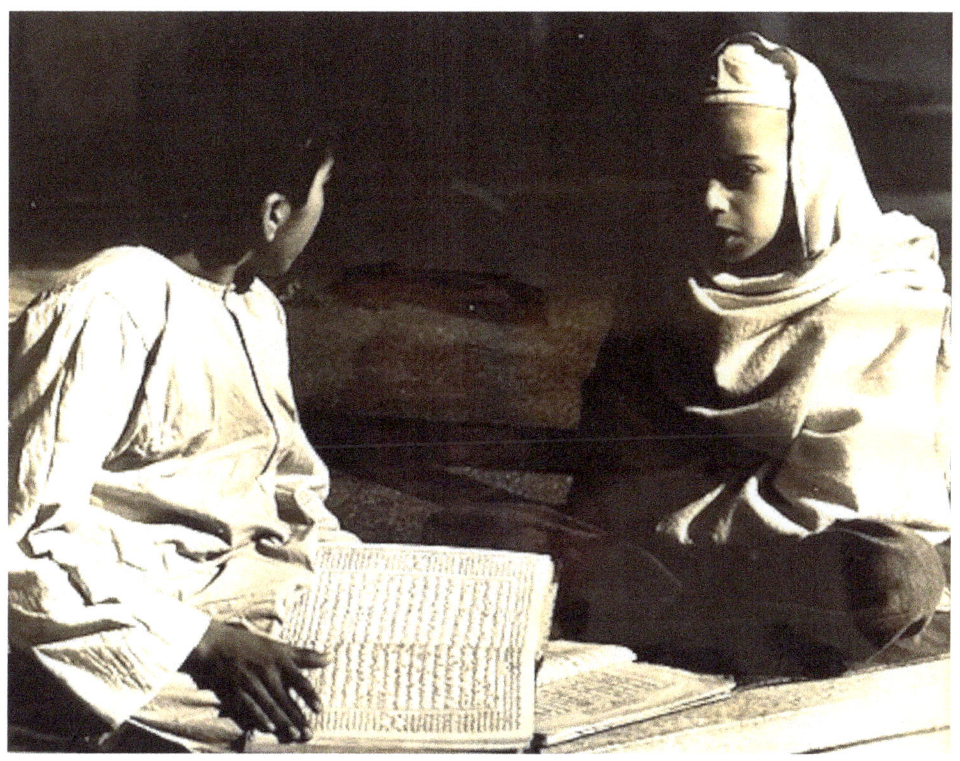

Boys memorising the Koran.

CHAPTER NINETEEN

COCHIN

Cochin, also known as Kochi, was the first main contact point in India for European explorers. It became known as the centre for the spice trade and this attracted foreigners. It was known to Arab sailors, Greeks and Romans. It also attracted many Jews. Portuguese explorers were here in the 1400s. But the earliest record is from a book by the Chinese voyager, Admiral Zheng He, in the same century. The Portuguese navigator Pedro Álvares Cabral founded the first European settlement on Indian soil at Kochi in 1500.

Anthony Harrop and I, together with local colleagues Thomas Matthew and Zach Koshy, went to the small Bolgathi Island. They were keen to keen for us to see the Bolgathi Palace Hotel where I was to speak at a conference of Bible Society workers. I describe it in my diary as 'a huge building with only six rooms.' Built in 1774 by the Dutch, it is the oldest Dutch palace outside of Holland. It has become a high class tourist centre.

The Apostle Thomas brough the Christian Gospel to East India and a church that bears his name is the largest in the State and is known as the Mar Thoma Church headed by a Metropolitan.

The Mar Thoma Church sees itself as continuation of the Saint Thomas Christians, a community traditionally believed to have been founded in the first century by Thomas the Apostle who is known as Mar Thoma (Saint Thomas) in Syriac, and describes itself as "Apostolic in origin, Universal in nature, Biblical in faith, Evangelical in principle, Ecumenical in outlook, Oriental in worship, Democratic in function, Episcopal in character".

Late in the afternoon a local dance group was brought in to entertain us. This the Kathakali the most well-known dance drama from Kerala. It means "Story-Play" said to be 1,500 years old. The dancers are elaborately made up and wear very colourful costumes. The dance teacher told us of the way children were trained from an early age and she particularly wanted us to observe the eye movements of their eyes. Nowadays its easy to see these demonstrated on the internet. Its quite incredible how the dancers can more their eyes in time with the music. Their training takes fifteen years.

That evening we had dinner at the home of a printer that often did work for the society. We usually were careful about accepting 'gifts and favours' from our printers, but 'he was a good man, quite above any sense of bribery,' we were told. Besides he was the only printer in the State that could manage a full thousand-page Malayalam Bible The food was absolutely beautiful. Like a mixed seafood platter of mussels, prawns, juicy fish fillets and delicious calamari rings with Kerala spices and chutneys! A traditional special meal was usually served on a coconut leaf but our host used a set of beautiful Edgewear crockery which, our hostess proudly said, 'was bought at Harrods in London.'

After taking a veritable feast the hostess announced that we must try the most famous Kerala dish – a prawn curry from the Malabar region. It was an incredible blend of spices, coconut milk, chilli, plus marinated prawns, drumsticks and raw mango. I've forgotten all of the spices used but I remember black mustard and fennel which were new to me.

The meetings went on for three days culminating in opening a Bible kiosk at Ernakulam railway station. We had a meal at the YWCA – the Young Women's Christian Association. Chan Choi, our UBS regional secretary, when thanking the young women for the meal said, 'Sorry, but we are all too old for you.' Their representative gushed a response, 'Oh but you are our model men!' Incidentally, we found that there was always a ready sale of Bibles at railway stations.

The final day of the conference was addressed by the UBS leaders. I was officially appointed as the Honorary Information Consultant to the Bible Society of India.' As my diary notes, 'I was to help prepare a special set of Scripture Selections, a really important step.'

The final day of the visit saw us taking a cruise on the backwaters of Cochin including a visit to the Chinese fishing nets.The Chinese fishing nets – Cheenavala in Malayalam – are believed to have been introduced in Kochi by Chinese explorer Zheng He, from the court of the Kublai Khan. The fishing net system was established on the Kochi shores between 1350 and 1450 AD. I think the technical name is shore operated fishing nets. They are up to 20 metres high and 10 metres across.

The backwaters are a labyrinthine system formed by more than 900 kilometres (560 miles) of waterways. Its such a peaceful experience to glide along the streams through forests and fields of crops. Especially when paddled by silent men and not have a noisy outboard motor. Before this though, some of the group wanted to go for a swim but when I saw the dirty oily water I chose to sit it out and chat with my colleague Victor Itty.

I was travelling in India with John Dean of the United Bible Societies and visited the town of Adur in Kerala, South India. A group of men came to visit us and they each had a story to tell. One young man named Subrahmanian was keen to tell us of his conversion to Christianity but he told it such a matter of fact way his words did nothing to convey the tragedy of his life since becoming a Christian. "I am 20 years old and come from a Hindu Brahman family. When I was in college a friend gave me a New Testament and I began to read it secretly. I did not want my father who is a Hindu priest to know as I often helped him in the temple.

"After ten months I became convinced of the truth I was reading and accepted Christ as my Saviour. My family was greatly angered and began to create many problems for me. When they could see that I would not turn away from my new Christian beliefs they kicked me out of the house.

"But my faith is strong and I get a lot of support from my Christian friends. I want to receive a theological education and will soon be going to the seminary."

Mathews M Kurian wants to dedicate his life to the ministry of Bible translation. "I took a Bible correspondence course which changed my life," he said. "This caused me to examine the Bible very carefully and I discovered for myself that this is the true Word of God. "I have a BSc and MSc in mathematics and have now switched to the study of Hebrew and Greek. There are two reasons why I want to do Bible translation. Firstly, only God's Word can really change a person. Secondly, the Bible tells us that at the end there will be a huge crowd from every nation and kindred around the throne praising God. I want that to come true, and for this to happen, people from every nation must hear the news."

Raji Joseph said, "I come from a Hindu background and a very poor family. My father and mother never knew God, and there were many quarrels. When I was five years old my mother left us and went to live with her parents. We children grew up, and after five years we went to persuade her to return, which she did.

"But all this disruption caused much pain in my life. I would come home drunk and fight with my parents. Then I left home and went to work in a liquor shop. However in the meantime my parents came to know Christ and started praying for me. On 15th August, 1994 I myself became a Christian after a man gave me a New Testament. He showed me the different parts of the book and suggested that I first read the one by John. I was fascinated from the first sentence and read it right through from beginning to end in one night. What I read so stunned me that I knew right away that this was the spiritual truth I was looking for and I became a believer in Jesus Christ. I read the whole book of John in one night. What a great gift from God! Last year I started studying at Paranthal Bible College.

One of the Cochin pastors was keen to chat with me. He was soon telling me of his experiences counselling his people. His wife brought a young woman to meet me and asked her to tell me her story which I recorded.

> 'My boyfriend broke up with me. I am just busying myself meeting new people not for love but for friendship. I don't want to have a love relationship anymore. I am not lucky with that. I always fail. My parents chose an awful man for me. Even at first when I saw him, I didn't like him. I think he looked so, I think you call it, supercilious. So I was married in 1985 when I was at the age of 19. We had 4 kids. In 1992 we decided to get separated. I found another husband a year later. This time it was my choice. We had 2 kids. So I have 6 kids in total. Again, the relationship still did not work. I am a total loser. I can't blame anyone else but myself. Now, I am living on my own. Working hard supporting my 2 younger kids. Making sure they will not become starved. The other kids are living with their biological father. But I am supporting them including their father because he doesn't like to work. I have had a very bad life. They say arranged marriages are the best, but I don't believe it. Since becoming a Christian, I have learned that the Lord Jesus will guide me in the right paths so I'm reading the

> Bible very carefully. My pastor assures me that God's will is the best for me so I must wait for him to guide me.'

Coming from a railway family I have always loved trains and I travel on one whenever I can. My father received a gold badge for his 33 years of service to New Zealand Government Railways. His sons did another twenty years. As mentioned earlier, long-distant train travel in India is a great place to meet people. On one trip, my Indian colleague and I had reserved seats in a First Class a.c . When we boarded we found it packed full of young women. What to do? Call the guard. He soon came and sorted it out leaving us with three women and one man.

At the first stop they got off except one woman. My colleague chatted with her for a while and she was soon telling us her story. She was working as a house maid, and said, 'I have a sad story to tell you. I'm from a strict Hindu home. A boy who is my neighbour was very nice to me and always secretly smiled at me. One day my brother saw us exchange smiles and he was very angry. He told our parents and they became very angry, with father saying, 'If you carry on like that you will finish up dishonouring our family.' A week later my brother saw us again, exchanging smiles. We had not even exchanged one word, only a smile. But to him it was fornication.

He angrily grabbed me and dragged me inside the house and started to beat me with a broom. It was the usual small straw broom and didn't hurt very much but he beat me all over my body, even down the front on my breasts. Both parents we were out at the time.

'I was already 23 and they had done nothing about a husband for me. They just wanted me to be their servant. I suddenly thought there is no future here for me here. I was never left alone even for a minute. I went to my room and packed a small bag and waited for the chance to go out. I knew where mom kept her money hidden so I raided it and took it all, about one thousand dollars. I reminded my brother of something dad had asked him to do so he went out, saying he would be back in ten minutes but I must stay in the house. That was enough time for me to get out of the house and catch a rickshaw to the railway station. My hastily made plan was to take the next train no matter what its destination. I hoped it would be to a far part of the state where they spoke a different dialect to us, and leave my family for ever. I was so lucky as there was a train waiting to depart.

'I found a second class a.c. cabin with a spare seat. The family occupying it were from the far north and spoke Bhojpuri which is so different from my language. But there was one young man with them who was different and after an hour he began to speak to me in English and a bit of Bengali. Three hours later we had become friends. He had listened to my story and was very sympathetic and understanding. He was travelling to a place where he was to take up a job. 'Why don't you come with me?' he asked. 'I'm alone and an orphan and have no family.' My plan was to travel for several hours far away from my horrid family. So I followed him and we found a room and lived together, telling the landlady we were a married couple.

'He was so good to me. His boss found me a job as a nanny with his neighbour, and I was very happy. I loved being with him, and after a while I fell pregnant. He was shocked and said 'How can that be?' Stupid man! Surely he knew that after making love numerous times, that would happen. When I woke next morning he had gone, taking all his things. Later, when I checked his office, they said he had not come to work. After a week, his job was given to another. He appeared to have left the area.

'Now I am seven months pregnant. I'm living with another young woman who became my friend. She too had run away from her family who actually drove her out of the house when they found that she was with child, threatening to kill her if she stayed.

'We lived together for three years. Her baby is two years old now, and she has no work. So I have been supporting them, providing everything they need. I rent a room in cheap house for us. I suppose I like her baby because I lost mine at birth.

'I'm just like a husband and father to them. But I'm not a man. In my heart I am a girl. So don't get me wrong, we ourselves are not lesbians, at least I'm not. . I'm so stressed because even though I gave them everything, she cheated on me. She loves other girls and even brings them to our place. But she has no work so I'm the one who works for them. I can't leave her and her baby because I love her baby with all of my soul. I paid for everything during her pregnancy and when the baby came I provided the milk. But we fight too much but always I'm drawn to her baby.

'I decided I needed a man in my life. But a woman here can't go looking for a man. One day in the market I saw a man whom I knew. Incredibly, he was a classmate and we were both far from our original homes. That was eight months ago. He was a seaman and still single and was looking for a girlfriend so invited me to live with him. For one month he was so good to me. Then I have to confess that I said that we are a couple so it's all right to make love. He was fine until I told him I was pregnant. Next day he left, going back to his boat. He did not tell me anything but disappeared. I was able to call his best friend's sister and she told me he has already a family.' With the train stopped, she got off so we never heard the rest of her story.

One of the secretaries in the office I regularly visited could never do enough for me. When she discovered how I liked my tea or coffee she made sure I was never thirsty. In fact I was a little worried that this may cause talk in the office as relationships between men and women are so different in India. But I believe all was well. Her name was Anna and one day she told me that she had a sister that worked in the middle east for a couple of years and had recently returned home. Knowing that I was a writer she asked me if I would like to meet her and hear her story. Her husband was an railway engineer so that all made for an interesting visit to her home.

"My nick name is Joyjoy. But my nightmare came on March 31, 2014 when my husband came to the school where I teach, and in front of my class, he shouted at me about something and punched me in the stomach. That was terrible and I wanted leave and not go back to work there. I felt so shy before my students who witnessed what my husband did to me. Then one day I met a friend of my mum and she encouraged me to apply for a job overseas. There were many Indian women working in that area as maids and all kinds of work. I immediately decided to apply for a housemaid position in Kuwait. There was a great demand and I was appointed straight away. So I grabbed the opportunity, and without thinking well, I was on my way.

"I was soon in Kuwait as a domestic helper. For three months my employer was good with me but after that, she changed a lot. All the rules established by the Indian government for workers like me were broken. She took my passport, charged me for my food, did not give me a private place in which to sleep and never had a day off. Because it was my first time I'm afraid to ask for these things. I did not have my own room but slept in the sala. The door was locked every night.

"I had only five hours sleep because she said that I don't have the right to rest too much because she pays me lot money to work. So I usually got to sleep 3 a.m. and woke up at 8 a.m. and started working immediately. I was not permitted to rest during the day not even to eat breakfast or lunch. I was given one bread and tea at 4 p.m. – that was all was given and I had to eat and drink it standing. I took food from the fridge for my dinner and she carefully checked what I had and docked my salary. There was only stale chapatis or nan bread and usually there was very little protein. I was allowed one glass of distilled water before sleep. Otherwise I had to drink the dirty water from the tap.

"I was never allowed to sit down even for a minute. She checked everything I did and if she wasn't pleased she called me a donkey. I held my breath trying not to talk back as I keep in mind I'm there for the sake of my family. Prayer was my only weapon.

"When they go out, they take me, but I had to sit in the corner and was not allowed to look around or acknowledge any other maids there. There were always many maids there from different countries like Sri Lanka, India, Ethiopia, Somalia and the Philippines. I wasn't allowed to smile back at them but sit like a robot in a corner not allowed to look everywhere. The family would have a nice meal but give me nothing to eat. I could only smell the food, usually a delicious curry. They didn't even offer me water. Life was so hard, and I would say to myself I'm doing this for my family. If we went on vacation, I always slept on the floor as she said the housemaid deserve only to sleep there. I couldn't bring any personal things with me. Then I had to sleep in the kitchen. I cried a lot and begged her to let me talk to my family.

"When we came back from the market we would buy two tanks of gas but she would not allow me to use the elevator but had to climb all those stairs with those heavy things.

"I had to be very patient, but we maids are good at hiding our feelings, being willing to suffer saying everything will be ok in the end. After four months, I knew a lot of their language, so I knew what they were talking about.

"They are not human.

"However maybe not all of them."

Once when walking around the streets of Calcutta I began chatting with a small family that had settled on the footpath and had been there for several weeks. We didn't have a common language but I offered to take their photo, promising to give them a copy on my next trip. About a month later, I went to find them and found they had disappeared. I showed their photos to others there, but they shook their heads saying, 'They have gone.'

But so many of the people suffer very much from lack of income. When you have the chance to talk to them privately, it is so disturbing to hear about their problems.

BOMBAY BIBLE SOCIETY

Bombay was known to the Portuguese, back in 1538, when they called it Bom Bahia, Portuguese for 'Good Bay.' Mumbai, its present name, is from the Hindu religion. Ptolemy the Greek astronomer and geographer called it Heptansia – the city of seven islands in AD 150, so back then it must have been a significant place. These island are now joined together by causeways and bridges making them indistinguishable from each other.

In an effort to return to its roots, Bombayites decided to change the name of their great city to Mumbai, So now it's residents are called Mumbaikars or Mumbians. One reason was to be rid of names from the British Raj but to many people, this was a joke, because it was the name the first European colonisers gave it – the Portuguese.

I was leading a marketing seminar for the local staff plus a few volunteers and after a couple of days it was suggested that we go out onto the streets and sell Gospel booklets. The local language is Marathi, but in fact, practically all the languages spoken the country can be heard here. We were all given books in not just Marathi but a few in Gujarati, Hindi, Nepali and Urdu. Before going out onto the streets, the local manager gave a few tips about the people we were likely to meet. "Remember this is the most corrupt city in India: its home to more bandits, thieves, prostitutes and evil people of all types, including the police, than any other place in our country. So be very careful and respectful when you speak to any one.' I didn't tell him that a few days ago, being intrigued with the slum area, I took a walk through them. The people were very surprised but none failed to greet me. I gave away a few Marathi booklets and these were accepted courteously. I just said, 'Would you like a Christian book?' There were no refusals.

'Wow,' I thought, 'Is it wise to send all these young people out there, carrying what could be controversial literature?' But they took it all on the chin, and grinning to each other, agreed, 'Yes, that's our place.' Although I had read everything I could about Bombay, but there was much I didn't know or understand. In later years, reading books like *Maximum City*[14], or *Shantaram*[15], that gave vivid descriptions of this iniquitous city, made me realise how fortunate I was not getting into trouble.

There were two married couples present and one evening the manager invited me to have a meal with them and hear their amazing stories. Twin boys had married twin sisters. The women had come from an isolated village near the border of Nepal and China. Their mother was Nepali and father from a small tribe that practised polyandry, or two men were husbands to the same woman. This was strictly illegal but secretly practised by a small tribe in northern Nepal. They kept the woman busy because she produced twelve children in twelve years. But they were very poor and when a 'trader' from Bombay visited their village and showed how they could benefit if they sent two of the older girls to Bombay for work. He promised them sums of money that they could hardly visualise. In one week, one girl could earn as much as her father did in a year.

The father suggested he choose the best ones and he selected the eleven-year old twins, Babie and Bihanie. This was all so exciting for the family and amidst floods of tears from parents and siblings, they left the next morning. The girls clung to each other in fear and excitement during the 14-hour bus ride to Kathmandu. It was the first time out of their village and they marvelled at the size of the capital city. They slept outside in the grounds of a Hindu temple then proceeded by bus to Gorakhpur in India. They were handed over to a woman who welcomed them warmly and assured them that she would look after them.

The next stage of the journey was a 40-hour train trip in what used to be called 3rd class. It was called a stopping train as it stopped at all stations no matter how small and insignificant. Fortunately it wasn't over-crowded so they each had a wooden seat. But the train frightened them at first; they had never heard such a noise as the wheels click-clacked over the rail joints. Their guide had a

14 *Maximum City*, Reveir, Suketu Mehta.

15 *Shantaram*, Picador, Roberts.

traditional bedroll but the girls had to sleep on the hard seats. This was not a problem to them as they had never slept on anything but a thin straw mat on the floor. As one of them said, 'we were terrified and excited all at once, and we clung together for comfort.'

On arrival in Bombay they packed into a single rickshaw and taken to an apartment in a decrepit-looking building and told to wait in a small room that had only mats on the floor. They were brought water and a plate of rice and chutney and told to get some sleep. They collapsed onto the floor being utterly worn out by the long uncomfortable journey and slept for 16 hours.

In the morning their minder came to talk to them and explain their work. They possessed only two sets of clothes that were very old and worn. A tailor was brought in and he measured them for blouses and showed them samples for saris. The madame said to him, 'Remember they will grow much bigger soon so make sure they fit.' As usual, when measuring women, he did not put the tape measure against their chests but guessed the size.' Their work was to clean the four apartments on the floor for this they should wear their old clothes. The new ones were for the special clients they would meet later. They were too nervous and frightened to ask about the clients.

After a week their boss came and handed them some new clothes, a blouse and a sari. 'You wear these when you are cleaning,' they were told. Give me all your old clothes, they are not fit for the city. Change now. Give me all of them including underclothes.'

'But there are no undies here,' said Babie.

'You don't need them here.'

'It was at that moment that I began to fear what they intended of us,' said Bahinie.

A year later, when they had both matured, they were taken to a nearby apartment and introduced to the woman in charge. 'You call me Madame,' she said. 'You must do everything I tell you to do. First of all put on these new clothes the tailor has made for you.'

Babie explained that as young girls, they always looked forward to the time when they would wear women's clothes like bras and pantries. 'So we were very puzzled when the Madam said we didn't need them in this new job.' They were taken to a small room that had one large bed and nothing else. Looking out the window they could see several women sitting near the windows of the apartments next door. The windows had several steel bars across them. Although they didn't know it, these were the infamous cages of Bombay where prostitutes were kept.

One evening the Madame came and told the girls that their job was no longer cleaning but to work with men and make them happy. 'A man will come to you tonight so I want you to do everything he tells you. I know that you will feel frightened of him but after a while you will get used to this job.' A very rich diamond merchant, a regular client of this brothel, heard about the twins and offered a huge sum to be able to deflower them. He paid the Madame US$10,000. He turned out to be quite gentle with them, and as their husbands explained, 'He didn't hurt them very much and a doctor was called in next day to examine the girls. He declared that they weren't damaged, only deeply traumatised by the experience and recommended they be rested for three days.' Some estimates say that about 40% of all prostitutes are from Nepal because they are fair skinned and compliant.

Because they were so young, for their first five years, the madame permitted them to see only three men a night. They worked every day with three days off per month. They had left home in such a hurry they did not know the address of their parents so were unable to communicate with them. It wasn't until after being married a year were they able to go back to their home.

One day when out shopping with a minder they were given a small packet of books by a young girl. These were Gospel Packets produced by the Bible Society in India. They contained the *Gospel of Luke* and several leaflets about various subjects in Hindi. When they told the young woman that they could only read Nepali, she quickly switched the packet for one in their language. Actually, these girls had never been to school but were taught to read by their father. 'We read every word again and again until finally we agreed that they were the truth.' Together they decided to become followers of Jesus.

Three months later when they were on their monthly visit to the market for just an hour . One day they found a group of young people singing about Jesus. This astounded them. An older woman with the group began to talk to them and when she discovered that they were new believers asked them where they came from. She immediately realised that they were captives from the Falkland Road cages let out for an hour or two. Two of the young men were told to escort them to their church and two of the strongest looking men were asked to grab the minder hand her over to her first policeman they saw. They very sensibly did this very quietly without creating a disturbance. The minder herself quickly understood what was happening and allowed herself to be led few metres to a policeman standing nearby.

The Marathi pastor whose wife was a Nepali was able to carefully counsel them. She led them in prayers of confession of the evil things they had been forced to do and guide them along a path of righteousness. They had a spare room in their house and invited the girls to live with them. The warmth and love extend to them by all the thirty members of the church almost overwhelmed them. 'We've so many aunties now, and uncles.'

Twin young men at the church became very interested in them. They were orphans having lost all of their family in riots in the city a few years ago in 1992 when about a thousand people died. This family had lived in a large complex comprising several houses that accommodated the entire family. They were invaded by Hindu extremists who killed everyone in the compound, the entire family and all their servants. They totalled about 45 people. So without parents or uncles to assist, they were actively looking for brides. Within minutes of first meeting them, they said to each other, 'We've found them! They are twins, they are lovely and they are saved!' ' Six months later they were married.

The pastor's wife introduced me to a young woman, saying 'she's got story.'

> "My name is Christine and from that you can tell that I am a Christian. But my family is not a good example of what Christians should be like. When I was seven years old, my parents separated. My mother has now got a new family. My dad too has a new family. So I was given to my grandmother who brought me up.
>
> "And at the age of 16, I had a secret boyfriend. He made me pregnant so we began to live together. My grandmother was becoming quite weak and ill and didn't care about me and was glad I was out of her hands. There were no family men to control me. We continued our relationship and we had another child. So we decided

get married. We delayed this because we had to find the money to pay for a marriage in the church.

"We were together almost two years when I realised that my husband was being unfaithful to me. We were still members of the church but the problem was that there were so many people there who, although they called themselves Christians, were not true believers and followers of Christ. A true Christian obeys all the teachings of Jesus Christ but there were some women who did not do that. One of them seduced my husband.

"We knew already that we did not truly love each other but I was just thinking of my kids, and felt I had to keep our family intact because I don't want my kids to grow up without a father to guide them.

"But his cheating became too much. He worked in a bakery in another suburb and would come home for the weekend. But he began to miss some weekends and stayed where he worked. One day a lady told me that he had been living with another woman there.

"We decided to separate and for a while he supported our kids. But I've had no contact with him for a long time. I took work in the market so as to provide our daily needs like food. A friend of my granny became my aunty who had no children of her own, helped me by taking care of my children. She is such a lovely Christian. I'm pleased with myself that I can do something to help my little family. But it's a struggle to find the money for their school like books, pens, a school bag and uniforms.

"In 2021 I was diagnosed with kidney failure. I was in hospital for almost two weeks and was seriously ill. The aunty took care of the kids. I can say that I was not frightened to die because I had been saved by Jesus and I trusted him as my saviour. But I just have to worry about my children. I had an operation and was on dialysis for five months. Nowadays I can't lift anything heavy so I sell a few vegetables and some fruit. This is mostly fruit from auntie's garden. We pay an elderly man to keep it for us. He has no family and sleeps in a shed and tells me that he is very happy to have a small job that gives him enough to buy his rice.

"The money I earn is enough for our food and medicine. But recently my little daughter got ulcers on both legs around the knees and needed proper treatment. When I went to the hospital they would not even let me in the door until I paid about two hundred dollars. I begged them but they said it was the rule of the hospital. I went back again the next night but still no success. The security guards said, 'No pay, no treatment.' All I could do was to go to a money lender. It took a long time to clear that debt."

That evening after supper the pastor said that he has asked another person to see me and tell her story about the power of God's word in her life. The team met her when they were selling books.

"Call me Sue, because my real name is difficult to say. I come from a religious and conservative Hindu family. I was 15 years old when my father and mother separated. They kept their story hidden for years. I think it was my father's fault. He was working overseas in some kind of labouring job in Doha and cut himself off from the family. My mother became a very bitter woman. She always favoured my elder sister and treated me like dirt. Nothing would please her. I decided to leave the them and waited for my chance to escape from the house. I wrote a simple note that just said, "I'm leaving." I was only 15 years old when I took the train to Bombay. I soon got a job in a Bombay club as an entertainer. I had no more interest in my family and decided to stand alone and live on my own.

"I tried to finish my study but I failed to do this. I finished secondary school all right but I failed my university exams. Actually all my life has been a failure. The entertaining job was very risky because that club attracted all of kinds of people, both men and women who lived only for entertainment and doing all kinds of evil things. I met a man and he became my boyfriend and he soon made me pregnant. But he was a married man so had no future for me. I took a second boyfriend who gave me another baby. But he became a drug addict. He introduced me to drugs. But the relationship didn't work out because he's an uncontrollable addict.

"Drugs are such a terrible curse and he began to hate me and that made him set me up by leaving drugs at my place then reporting me to the police. I was convicted and sent to jail even though I was five months pregnant with his baby. I gave birth inside the jail and that was a terrible experience. Thy wouldn't let me even see or touch the baby.

"Then after a year in jail, they let me out. None of my family wanted to see me because they thought I was such a bad person. The club was willing to take me back because I still looked good and retained my figure. After singing and dancing there were always men who wanted me to go with them for the rest of night. I made lots of money but inwardly I was so sad and unsatisfied.

"Then one day at the market some people were selling books. They had them in several languages including my own, Gujarati. I didn't realise they were about Christianity otherwise I would never have bought them. One leaflet called *Are you Satisfied?* I certainly wasn't satisfied with my life. This man was writing about all the things he had, and he had more than anyone else, and he still wasn't happy. Lots of money, possessions and women – he had everything. Another small book called Mark explained who Jesus Christ was. I thought I knew about him because some of my people worshipped him along with all the other gods. My aunty had him on her altar shelf. I read all of the book in one night. Right at the end of the book, the last words were about his message and that through it people could be saved forever. So I became a believer. The next thing was to find some other believers that I think were called Christians. It didn't take long to find some and one nice lady gave me such a warm welcome and had taught me so much about my new faith."

There was another woman keen to tell her story. 'Meet Sunita,' said the pastor's wife. She has something to tell you.'

> 'My name is Sunita. I am 34 years old. I had to leave home when I was still a teenager because my brother accused me of bringing dishonour on the family. He saw me talking to a boy after my college class. We were on the street not hiding away but he thought that it was disgraceful. 'You don't talk to boys unless we arrange it,' he said. He was a nice boy and we certainly were not talking about getting married. When my mother heard about it she screamed at me. Father took a broom and began to beat me. He was so angry he hit me all over my body all down my back and my chest and stomach. It was several days before I could stand up and walk. As soon as I could, I escaped from them one night and went to a Christian school friend. Her mother took me to her doctor who gave me some comforting balm. She put it on me and after three days I felt much better. Her father gave me some money and the address of a Christian family in Bombay. They took me to the railway station and made sure I got on the right train. Her father called his friends and explained my situation.
>
> 'So I was free for a while and found a job with a company. They wanted to transfer me to Poona and I quickly settled in there. An office mate became very friendly and it wasn't long before we began to live together. We were both far from any relatives and could please ourselves in what we did or how we lived out lives. He had a sad story too and been thrown out of his home and family. After three years I had two kids but I raised them alone since my partner left me for another woman then was killed in a motor bike accident. None of his family were at his funeral. He would never tell me what his problem was except that it was something about an aunty. But after I gave birth to our second daughter he cheated on me. I actually saw him having sex with another woman because I came home early from work one day and found them on our bed bound together.

'Then I met a guy and we were both fell in love. I truly loved with him and trusted him. We made love many times and then I fell pregnant with my third daughter. I was so happy but then I discovered that he was cheating me. He was the man I used to trust and I discovered he was married to another woman. It was too late because I was pregnant. Depression enveloped me. That day I began to feel so distressed and I came to the point of wanting to end my life. But then I thought of my kids and how they depended on me so I thank god I'm still alive.

'I'm thankful for the good and bad memories of my life. I have to let God take care of me. The past it past. Perhaps it was a good thing I never got married to either of them so if God brings a suitable man into my life I will be able to marry hm.

'As I thought about everything, I knew that I could not go back to my Hindu family. They wouldn't want to know me so I made contact with the Christians who helped me. When I turned up on their doorstep I was overwhelmed by the way they welcomed me and my three small children. I had a lot of explaining to do, but they simply said, 'We know what you need. You need a saviour.' During the next few weeks they patiently explained the way of salvation and I accepted it and became a Christian.

'A few months later a widowed doctor and member of their church invited me to be his wife. He had no children and adopted my three, so we have become a family.'

CHAPTER TWENTY

THE BIBLE SOCIETY IN INDIA

'I think the best way to describe our work is that we are the largest user of paper in the country. We use more paper than the government!' Said the man in charge of printing the vast number of Scripture editions for India. My job is to keep in print Bibles in 14 languages and the New Testament in an additional 92 languages. Plus many millions of copies of the Gospels in a couple of hundred languages. Thus the Bible Society in India and is considered the largest publishing organisation in the country.

The languages of this single country are very complex. Well over a billion people share fifteen major state languages and another 220 minor ones. Plus a plethora of dialects. For example there are said to be 57 dialects of Hindi, Rajasthani has 73, Bihari another 34. In counting the number of languages there has always been the problem of deciding what is a language or a dialect. Twenty-four languages have more than one million speakers each.

Between all these tongues are eleven different scripts. English has become the lingua franca. Attempts have been made to make Hindi the national language but violent opposition from the southern people prevented that. So English remains the unofficial official language of India. Every five years a general election is held thus preserving the democratic status that was introduced at independence and preserved by the 22 semi-autonomous states. That so many vastly different people of a multiplicity of customs and culture, to say nothing of their differing languages, should be able to remain united in a single country, is an on-going modern day political miracle.

The work of the Bible Society is to publish the Christian Scriptures in the languages of the country. This has been going since 1811. They now publish the Bible in 140 languages.(this includes old versions, re-edited versions, revised versions, Common Language versions and first time publications covering 74 languages. New Testaments published now stands at 98 languages. (this number includes first time and updated versions representing 92 additional languages.

As an aside it is interesting to note that the BSI celebrates International Translation Day as prescribed by the United Nations.

> Language is a means of communication. The International Translation Day is a special day in the history of translation of the Bibles. It is a day to pay our tribute to the translation work done by our language professionals, and the translators. The task of translation plays an important role in bringing nations together, facilitating dialogue, understanding and cooperation, contributing to development and strengthening world peace and security. On 24th May 2017, the resolution approved by the General Assembly of the United Nations was to commemorate the role of language professionals and the translators. Thus, the United Nations declared 30th September as the International Translation Day.
>
> Generally, on 30th September the United Nations celebrates the feast of St. Jerome, one of the pioneers of the Bible translators, who is considered the patron saint of translators. St. Jerome was a priest from North-eastern Italy, who is known mostly for his endeavour of translating most of the Bible into Latin from the Greek. He also translated parts of the Hebrew Gospel into Greek. Jerome died near Bethlehem on 30th September AD 420. Thus, to remember this great saint Jerome and his contributions towards the translations, we, the members of the Bible Society of India are gathered together to celebrate this special day dedicating our present language professionals and the team of Translation into God's hand for the extension of God's reign.

I was able to travel to all major parts of India except Goa, Dar Jeeling, the Andaman Islands and some of the North Eastern States that were prohibited to foreigners like Nagaland.

This illustrates one of the big problems of travelling in India. There are so many wonderful sights and things to see and, of course, the people. But it is possible to spend weeks as tourists there, meeting only courteous hotel staff or friendly waitresses, and maybe a helpful taxi driver. But not really meet the people and learn about their lives. At the same time, it can be very frustrating to have the feeling that everyone is trying to rob you or take advantage of your 'wealth.' What seems like overcharging is sometimes misunderstood being in a society that thrives on bargaining. If a rickshaw driver in Calcutta says the fare is twenty rupees, in reality, he only expects you to pay ten! When the airport porter asks for twenty rupees a bag, he will be satisfied with ten – although he might be unhappy that he could not squeeze a bit more out of you – not being able to get what would be a day's wages for ten minutes work! The hotel porter might scowl when you offer what you know to be the correct tip of say, fifty cents, when he was expecting a dollar or even five!

But if you are a Christian, to meet people at a church is sure to be a wonderful experience. I always found them to be friendly and hospitable, even if they did not know who I was. Christians call each other brothers and sisters because they are all in the family of God.

Doctor Singh was a gentle kind-looking man, now in his seventies. He invited me to tea saying that he had a story to tell me. 'You know I'm a doctor and have given my life to help and heal people. We are sworn to help everyone, no matter who they are, or where they come from, or what they believe. But I have to say that there is one group I had difficulty with and that's the Christians. I was brought up as a Hindu and had a firm belief in its teachings.

One day when visiting a friend in a small town but the hotel I was to stay in was closed due to a strike, so I stayed in the home of my friend's friend. They were very kind to me and gave me a private bedroom. But that evening I couldn't sleep so I got up and tried to find something to read. There were no books or newspapers. I opened a drawer and found a book. It was quite thick and I opened it at random and found some poetry. They were beautiful words of praise to the gods. Yes, I thought, I worship this god. It explained beautifully all he does for us humans. So I got back onto the bed and read the remarkable words of chapter eight:

Our Lord and Ruler,
your name is wonderful
everywhere on earth!
You let your glory be seen[b]
in the heavens above.
2 With praises from children
and from tiny infants,
you have built a fortress.
It makes your enemies silent,
and all who turn against you
are left speechless.
3 I often think of the heavens
your hands have made,
and of the moon and stars
you put in place.
4 Then I ask, "Why do you care
about us humans?
Why are you concerned
for us weaklings?"
5 You made us a little lower
than you yourself,[c]
and you have crowned us
with glory and honor.
6 You let us rule everything
your hands have made.
And you put all of it
under our power—
7 the sheep and the cattle,
and every wild animal,
8 the birds in the sky,
the fish in the sea,
and all ocean creatures.
9 Our Lord and Ruler,
your name is wonderful
everywhere on earth![16]

I turned over many pages and came across stories of Jesus Christ. Goodness me! This is the Christian's book. For all my life I wouldn't dare read it. But I was astonished how beautiful it was. I read all

16 Psalm 8, Contemporary English Version @ American Bible Society, 1995.

night and by morning I was anxious to speak to my host about it. He kindly showed me how I could become a Christian. At first I was glad that I didn't have to go to a church to be converted. In the past I had joined groups who create a disturbance outside a church while they were worshipping like throwing stones on the roof. Now I spend as much time as I can reading this book and I've got copies in the five languages I know. It is interesting how each one is different, yet the same.

JAINISM

One day my colleagues suggested they take me to see the great Jain statue a few kilometres away. This was of Bahubalo, considered to be the first man to achieve liberation Jain style. This stone statue stands at the top of a hill that appears to be of solid rock. It is 17 metres high (62 feet) carved out of a single piece of rock reached by climbing a number of steps that seem difficult to count. I've seen references to them as being 614 steps carved out of solid rock to 650. When I climbed them, I easily beat all of my party to the top I but lost count of the steps. I was pleased with myself in being able to climb all those steps without stopping for a breather. Every 12 years, and unpronounceable in the English tongue, the Mahamastakabhisheka ceremony takes place. The giant 1,000 year old statue is bathed in milk and all kinds of precious food like saffron, sugarcane juice, sandal paste, rice flour plus flowers. I was told that entire 'hill' was solid rock with the statue actually part of the rock. It was carved in 983AD – an incredible feat of engineering.

Priests at the top of the hill told us to get rid of all leather items. 'What do I do with my belt?'

'Just put it over there and not let it get too close to Balubalo.'

'What about your wallet. Is it leather?'

'No, plastic.'

This statue commemorates the first man to achieve liberation. That is, liberation from all constraints of personal and public life. This liberation refers to being completely freed of all constraints of living, physical, sexual, spiritual and material. It is said that it is impossible for a women to achieve this.

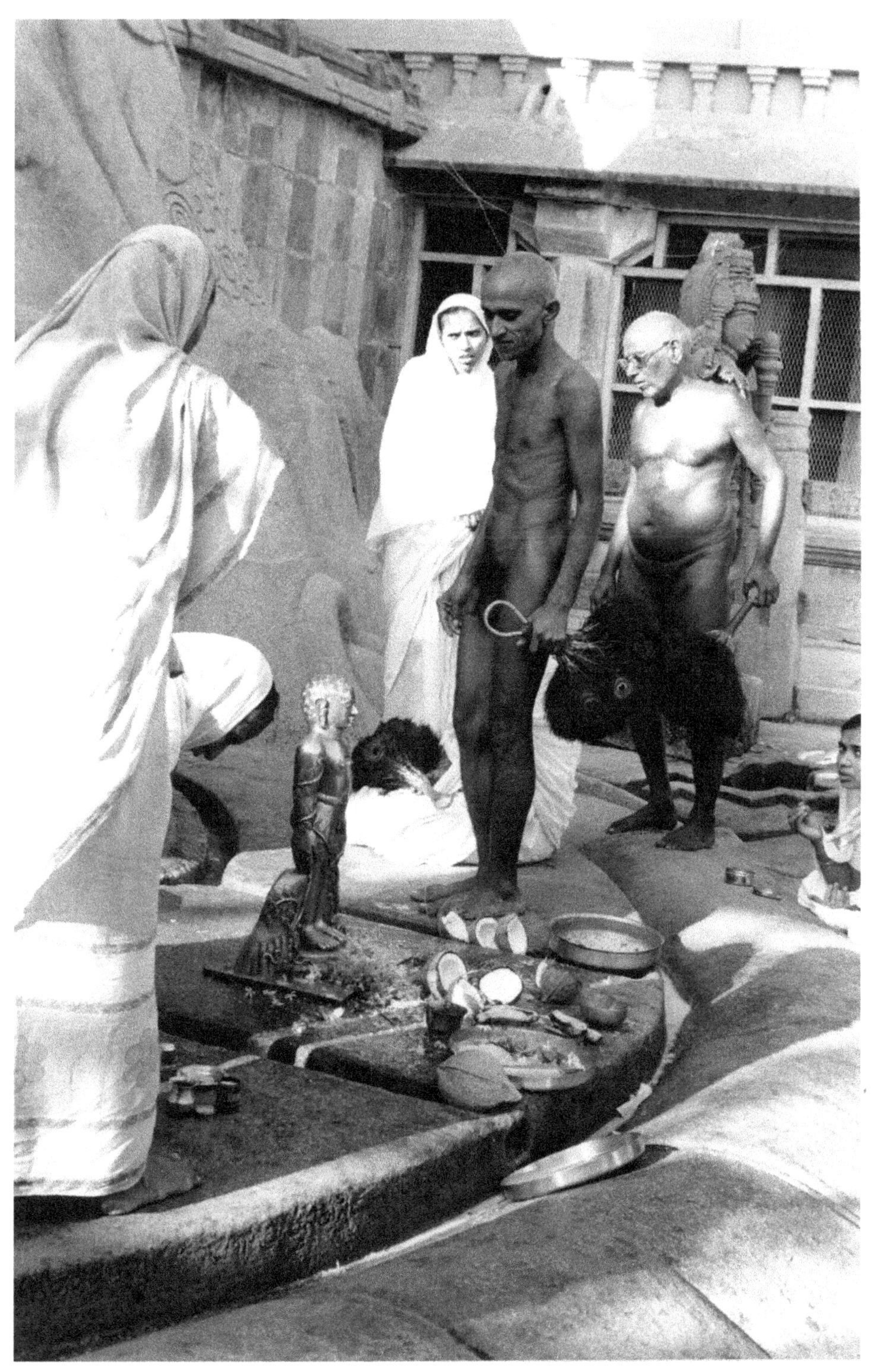

Jain pilgrims, Gommateshwara, Karnataka.

This was not an auspicious day so there were few people about. Two women were worshipping at his feet, caressing his big toe with great affection. 'Did you notice,' said one of my friends, ' that those women never looked up and stare at his foot long thing, but only patted and kissed his feet?' There were two men looking on who had given up everything, including their clothes. They were stark naked. They would have been through the diksha ceremony when they would have given away all their worldly possessions, including their money, and lived as monks or holy men.

These men are fanatical about not destroying any form of life. Like only ever drinking well water because all other types have tiny living microbes in it. In the wet season they stay inside and never walk through a puddle. They never take a bath. Some carry a small feather duster to clean every place where they sit. A Jain friend explained to me that the five vows they take, if they are serious about their religion, are: no violence, no untruth, no stealing, no sex and no attachments. Married people who have taken diksha often leave each other and their families for ever. But its like all other religions, people keep only the precepts they like. Such as some Christians who drink only water and others who take a whisky every night! There are Muslims, albeit devout, who rarely pray, let alone pray five times a day as prescribed by some leaders.

The police had set up a road block because there was a smallpox epidemic and were not letting people past without a vaccination. My colleague did not have his health passport with him. There were inspectors on both sides of the car so after mine was checked I swiftly passed it over to him and he handed it the man on his side, who waved us through.

HINDUSTANI

Although I have attempted to learn three languages seriously, and fiddled about with a couple of others, I never tried to learn Hindi or Hindustani. I knew it would be difficult because missionary candidates whom I knew were required to do two years of language study before beginning work. Besides I was all over the country often in non-Hindi areas. English is the unofficial official language. The government has never been able to proclaim it the official tongue and thus raised the ire of much of the country. Reading through Mohini Rao's *Teach Yourself Hindi didn't* inspire me especially when he suggested his was the easy way to learn Hindi! 'The easy way!' There's nothing easy about learning a language. That makes as much sense as a couple of other language books I have like '*Learning Tagalog in One Week*' or '*Korean in a Hurry.*' Any language has to be learnt correctly else all kinds of mistakes and misunderstandings will occur. Like in Hindi, the word '*dal*' can mean either lentils or a branch of a tree, depending on the pronunciation. '*Din*' can mean day or poor. Here's an interesting one – '*maatr*' means either poor or mother. Is this the origin of our word 'mother?' Coming from Sanskrit through Latin. '*Shur*' is either brave man or blind man. 'There are 11 vowels and 35 consonants in the Devanagari or Hindi script.' Said one English young fellow learning the language, 'and it took me two weeks to learn just that!' When discussing this with one of our translation consultants he explained that Hindi is written in Devanagari script, which is made of two Sanskrit words: *Deva,* meaning 'God' and *Nagari,* meaning 'origin'. So it is said by some Hindus that this method of writing is from God and must be greatly respected. Or as one writer put it, 'It's the language of God in the language of men.'

One young fellow training to be a missionary wrote about his experience of learning the language:

The script was so totally different, it took a lot of memorizing and practice to write. The sounds were so difficult to distinguish at first but soon I realized that every sound had its own letter, unlike English letters that can be pronounced several ways. I went to India to communicate the gospel so I knew I had to succeed. Listening to people and especially preachers, sure helped. But two years study was required and passing two formal exams! Thank God I passed and of course it became more and more easy.

THE FOOD

For several years we lived in a small English village along the Thames River between Oxford and Reading and one distinctive feature of this ancient town was the fact that there was no Indian restaurant there. The residents somehow felt that it did not suit them Every city and town has one but not Goring-on-Thames when we lived there. But that is an indication how widely Indian food is accepted in the United Kingdom. Some believe that curry is the most popular dish in Britain today. Its interesting to note that the word curry is an

English word transliterated from the Tamil *ka* meaning sauce.

I've met many people who have a fear of going to India because of the possibility of those hideous words Delhi Belly – an upset stomach accompanied by diarrhoea. Those who get amoebic dysentery never forget it. The rich food can upset some tummies and even the change of water, albeit quite pure, can be upsetting. But poor hygiene, and impure water is the greatest problem. But I kept strictly to the rules, no salads, no raw tomatoes, peeled fruit, not even the good-looking juice extracted from sugar cane on the street, or anything uncooked, and definitely no water. Even when a kindly hostess gave the assurance that water was boiled. No ice cubes in Pepsi Cola.

One of the golden rules about safe travel is not to drink the water. At that time good safe bottled water was not available everywhere. Even when bottled water was on sale, it was important to check that the lid was sealed because it might have been refilled from a tap. My policy was never to drink even boiled water but always tea or coffee. The strange thing was that water could be taken from a well, boiled yet still upset the tummy. Take the same water, make tea of it, and it would be quite safe. I rarely had a mild upset tummy and always had Imodium or Diamide Relief in my camera bag. One time when travelling with Henk Duym, a Dutch colleague, we had lunch with a medical doctor in Peshawar. When she placed a gleaming glass jug of cold water half filled with ice cubes on the table, she smiled broadly and said, 'the water is boiled and safe to drink.' My friend looked at it eagerly but first glanced at me. I quietly signalled 'No. Don't drink it.' But he couldn't resist and had two full glasses. Next morning when we met for breakfast he looked as white a sheet. 'I couldn't sleep last night,' he said. 'I spent the time on the toilet.' I was tempted to say 'I warned you.' But quietly said, 'Always drink the tea.' He missed out on a very exciting day miserably lying down. True, she might have boiled the water, even the ice cubes water.

Seated next to a businessman on Thai International travelling to Calcutta one day, we discussed the great food of India. 'I usually keep well,' he said, 'because I always brush my teeth with whisky.'

'But even that's not always possible because there are four dry states in India.'

His answer, 'I keep out of them.'

But I followed this rule in all tropical countries. I once engaged a film crew in the Philippines. For seven days I watched what they ate and drank like, no ice in their coca cola, no ice cream, no raw salads etc. On the last day I said, 'Today is our last day and you can eat and drink whatever you like today. The producer happily drank coke with ice all day and caught a plane that evening. Next day he wrote to me after getting home to the USA saying, 'I suffered all the way home and couldn't eat the good-looking airline food and I'm still crook.'

I was stopped in the street the other day by a collector for Medecins Sans Frontieres – Doctors Without Borders, and was asked what is the greatest killer of children in Asia? I guessed malaria. But no, the answer is gastroenteritis – caused by impure water.

The fact that the climate is often very hot and humid it is important to drink plenty to avoid dehydration. Pepsi cola is a good safe drink as is tea and coffee. Unfortunately, Coca-Cola was chucked out of India in 1977. This was considered, to be not just safe, but a good tummy settler albeit cooled in a fridge, not by ice!

A few years ago there was an English cricketer, their star wicket keeper, who would never touch the local food but ordered steak and chips for every meal twice a day for the entire tour of several weeks in India. He kept well, and kept wickets brilliantly!

The majority of the people being Hindus are strict vegetarians and have been so for centuries. In 296 BC the Emperor Ashoka banned the slaughter of any living animal and thus the people changed their diet. But even someone like me who has eaten all kinds of meat all his life, must admit to the huge range of delicious vegetarian food available in India.

This illustrates one of the big problems of travelling in India. There are so many wonderful sights and things to see and, of course, the people. But it is possible to spend weeks as tourists there, meeting only courteous hotel staff or friendly waitresses, and maybe a helpful taxi driver. But not really meet the people and learn about their lives. At the same time, it can be very frustrating to have the feeling that everyone is trying to rob you or take advantage of your 'wealth.' What seems like overcharging is sometimes misunderstood being in a society that thrives on bargaining.

But if you are a Christian, to meet people at a church is sure to be a wonderful experience. I always found them to be friendly and hospitable, even if they did not know who I was. This is because

Christians consider themselves to be born into God's family, so they all become brothers and sisters.

MARRIAGE

Seated next to me on a flight to Bombay was a fine looking businessman who asked about my visit to India. In turn I asked him what he had been doing in Madras. 'I'm looking for a bride for my son,' he said. 'He's 28 and time he was married.' He had seen an advertisement for a likely girl and had been to interview her and her parents. 'I prefer to do this myself rather than leave it to a marriage broker,' he said.

'What is your good name sir?' I asked.

'Patel.'

'Oh so you were looking for a nice Gujarati girl for your son?'

'Yes. True. But how did you know?'

'I've met a number of your people. Are there not plenty to choose from in Bombay?'

'No there's not. According to my wife, a Bombay girl is spoilt by modern living and would expect too much from her husband and his family. This girl I met is from a successful business family from a small town near Madras. She is neat and humble and has a BA and a BSC. I don't want a dowry: I don't need it.'

'And beautiful too?'

'Oh yes, she's beautiful enough but you will know that physical beauty doesn't last. I detect an inner beauty of the sort that is clearly evident in her mother.'

Westerners who don't practise arranged marriages, are often amused by the advertisements in newspapers. This one being quite unusual appeared in a BBC programme:

MATCH for opiniated
feminist. 30+ educated girl,
short hair, piercings, works in
social sector agnst cap'lism.
Wanted h'some, well built,
strictly 25-28 yr old only son
with estd business, bungalow/
at least 20 acre farm house.

Should know cooking. No
farters/ burpers plz. Write to
curbyourpatriarchy@

BANGALORE – BENGALURU

I was a frequent visitor to Bangalore where the Bible Society of India had its headquarters. This city has three nicknames – The Silicon Valley of India, The Garden City and the IT Capital of India. At 900 m.a.s.l. (3,000 ft) it has a comfortable tropical climate.

Among its many industries is printing. The Wesleyan Mission established the first press here in 1840. It has become a major print composing centre where the Bible Society arranged for Bibles and New Testaments to be composed in many languages of the world. These would be sent away for printing in perhaps Hong Kong or South Korea.

One evening in Bangalore, when work was finished and I was relaxing in my hotel room, there was a timid knock on my door. Even by that knock, I could sense it was someone with a problem that was a little scared to be visiting me. Somehow they had escaped the notice of the security guards who would never allow a visit without proper authorisation. I opened the door and there stood two young women, secretaries from the office. That they should be there was unheard of. They were either being very naughty or had a great problem.

I invited them in and offered them a glass of water. I began by saying, 'You shouldn't be here unless you have a huge problem.' She's got a big problem, sir, one we don't know what to do about it. We have come to ask your good self sir to tell us what to do. My friend here got married last month and her husband has been treating her bad.'

I answered I'm not the one to talk to about this. There are other people who will know what to advise. What about her mother, or aunty or sister? 'She is orphan sir. She has no one. You need to know how much she has suffered.' She then turned to her friend and pulled the sari off her shoulder and deftly undid the buttons of her blouse, and opened it. There was no bra. Her neck and upper chest were uncovered. They were a mass of bruises, as though strong hands had tried to choke her. She lowered the sari even more to reveal the top of her breasts. Her shoulder and neck were black and blue. Suddenly she pulled the cloth all the way down to her stomach. What had been beautifully shaped breasts were a mass of bruises. She had also been struck in the solar plexus several times, leaving huge marks.

This woman must have been a prize bride because she had what is commonly called wheaten skin. A beautiful wheat coloured light brown much prized by dark-skinned southerners. Her friend explained. 'Her husband is a very big black man, too big for her, very heavy, and...too big.' But why had she been brought to me? Then I remembered, two days ago when I was at the office I was struck on the hand by a falling piece of furniture leaving a bruise. I was helping to rearrange the furniture in the distributions team's office when someone let go of a desk and it crushed my hand. It immediately swelled up and discoloured. The office girls immediately rushed about looking for a bandage. I told them not to worry as I had something back at the hotel that would fix it. I always carried in my luggage a small tin of Rawleigh's white medicated ointment to deal with insect bites and bruises. That evening I used it on the large bruise that covered the back of my hand. The next day staff noticed that the bruise had gone and asked what I had done to it. These ladies must have heard about that and had come for treatment! When I began to say that I couldn't help her, they immediately reminded me of the way I had fixed the bruise on my hand. 'So please, sir, can we have it to fix this mess?'

It was such a small tin with hardly enough ointment to cover all those bruises. But I produced it and hoped it would help. The injured one thanked me profusely and bent to touch my feet in the traditional way of showing respect. But on straightening up she said, 'Your hands will have the spiritual touch sir, so please you put it on me.' Goodness me! If her husband heard that I had done that, he would come and give me more than a few bruises! I said to her friend, 'You have the gentle hands of a woman so you do it, and I will pray. Take it home and help her.'

'We can't do that sir, let's do it here now. He will find out. ' So I showed them the bathroom where they would have some privacy. It's a sad fact that domestic violence is a great problem in India.

It appeared that I was getting a reputation for helping people with their problems. In one of our offices a typist shyly asked me to meet her after work to talk about a problem. It would never do to meet her alone, so I asked a colleague to join us, that was, after asking her if that was ok. She agreed and I suggested she bring a friend.

We met in a café and she very quickly began her story. 'I have fallen in love with a man from Pakistan and I have suffered a lot because of that. Six years ago, I broke with my husband because he became unfaithful to me by having lots of girlfriends.

'A man from Pakistan found me on Facebook and became friendly with me. We chatted for about 9 months then he asked me to marry him. I felt that I was in love with him, and we discussed how we could do that. We became very serious about this. Then suddenly he told me that he was going to marry a girl his parents had found for him. This was to be in ten days' time. It was then that he confessed that he was engaged to her. I was very upset because we had become good friends and had even become quite intimate. He said he didn't want to tell me about his engagement because he thought I would leave him.

'But the problem is that he is a Muslim, however, seeing that I was a Christian, it was not a problem to him. They could arrange for a Nikkah (official Muslim marriage) online. After that I could join him. His idea was that we would live in a different city from his parents, but with his other wife. He did say that he could have four wives if he wants, and he's thinking that he would. But take one at a time!'

We discussed the problems that would arise if she went if she went ahead with the marriage. But she declared that because she loved him so much, all the problems would disappear.

My colleague and I had a long serious discussion with her and tried to assure her that it was best to avoid him in the future. Marriage like this would be sure to end in disaster. "But I have to say I am fond of him and he sends me a message every day and was still doing that ten days before his wedding. I don't want to offend him.'

I advised her that she shouldn't respond to his message on the same day as she usually did. But wait a day. Then next time wait two days. Never be in a hurry. He will finally get the message and you won't have offended or hurt him.

'That is so wise of you sir, thank you.'

SATELITES – INTO THE SPACE RACE

I was in the country at the time when it was announced that India's first satellite had been launched for them by the Russians in April 1975. It was designed and built in India and named after a famous Indian astronomer, Aryabhata. It was launched by the Soviet Union on 19 April 1975. Its purpose was to conduct experiments in X-ray astronomy, aeronomies, and solar physics. The spacecraft was a 26-sided polygon 1.4 m in diameter. All faces (except the top and bottom) were covered with solar cells. The newspapers had a field day lauding the cleverness of their engineers in making India the sixth country to enter the space age.

There were many letters of congratulations, but, at the same time, social workers decried this 'waste of money' when over half the population was still desperately poor subsisting on less than a dollar a day, even after thirty years of independence.

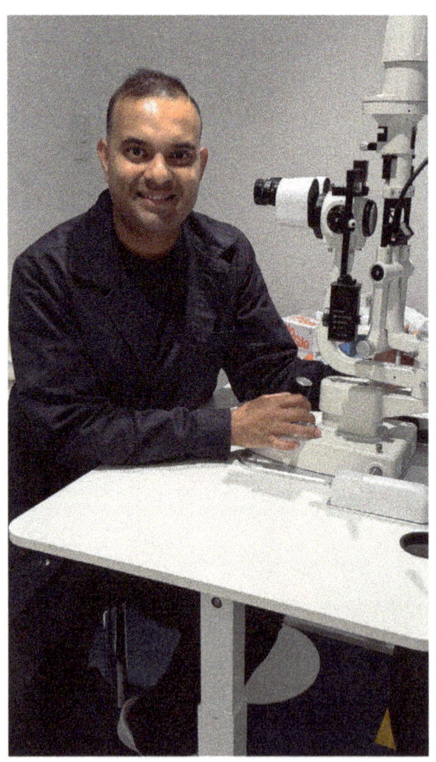

Optometrist Nath, whose Grand father was taken to Fiji in 1879 for work in the sugar plantations.
He now has a successful business in New Zealand.

CHAPTER TWENTYONE

DEMOCRATIC INDIA

India is by far the world's largest democracy. Every election sees 4,835 seats becoming vacant. One of the most amazing things is that a multiplicity of web sites will reveal the fact that a great number of elected parliamentarians have been convicted of crimes and or are under investigation. Here's piece written by Andrew North, the BBC South Asia Correspondent.

Published 15 February 2013

> According to the Association for Democratic Reforms (ADR), a Delhi-based campaign group, a third of India's 4,835 elected representatives have declared criminal charges against them – many of them face serious cases like murder, rape and kidnapping. The figures are based on information politicians themselves provide in their mandatory pre-election declarations.

Uttar Pradesh has more alleged criminals in its administration than any other state: one minister is among 29 of 58 ministers charged with some kind of crime. The state transport minister, is charged with attempting to murder a rival politician last year. He shows us the charge sheet drawn up by police, called FIR (First Information Report) in India. But the minister disputes whether he has been charged. "Maybe there is a complaint in a court or a police station," he says. "Maybe after an investigation, it might be found to be untrue." On his election declaration, he has admitted to other past attempted murder charges, as well as kidnapping and robbery.

So far, there has been no progress in any of these cases. One said everyone in his constituency knows about his rape charge, insisting that it is "a conspiracy" fabricated by rivals. That's possible in India's robust politics. But it can be rare for women to press charges of rape – especially in rural areas where tradition and caste govern life.

Like every other country in the world, India is changing. As one young person said, "We don't queue for anything anymore, we just click." As each generation comes, a certain number of traditions are lost.

YOUTH ARE CHANGING

India's aspiring middle class Gen Z – those between 18 and 25 years old – is making a break from tradition. But can the economy deliver on their dreams? Internet entrepreneur Ankur Warikoo has millions of YouTube and Instagram followers, and receives 300 emails a day from young people. Here is how he thinks the young Indians he has spoken to differ from their predecessors. (I asked for his permission to quote him.)

> "When we think of young, middle class Indians, we tend to think of them as hardworking, studious and largely respectful of their families' wishes and traditions. We imagine young men and women intensely prepping for competitive entrance tests that will earn them a spot in a top engineering or medical school. They are determined to chart a dependable careers for themselves and live out their parents' dreams.
>
> "This, of course, is a stereotype.
>
> "Many young middle class Indians that I've spoken to have questioned their parents, rebelled and trod alternative paths. They haven't always played it safe. But for the most part, even after a detour, they eventually buckled down and stuck to the script.
>
> 'Growing up, I was one of these people, and I believed that those who came after me were not that different. They wear different clothes and use different words (my 22-year-old video editor says it's way cooler to say "noice" rather than "nice"). They have more bars to go to, and perhaps have been in at least one romantic relationship before marrying. But I was sure that if I scratched the surface, I would find someone who was driven and aiming for a stable job.
>
> "But everything that I thought I knew about young middle class Indians was challenged when I started

creating content for them on YouTube and other social media two years ago. I have made videos that have been watched by more than four million young people – half of them are in the 18-24 age group, and 40% of them live outside of India's 10 biggest cities. They understand English but are more comfortable speaking in their native language. Every day, I receive hundreds of emails from them – topics range from money and careers to relationships and mental health.

"I have engaged with a 15-year-old self-taught coder; a college dropout who is helping his father take their family business digital; a 24-year-old painter who has been painting since the age of six; a freelancer who is already earning three times what he would have made from a full-time job straight out of college; and an accountant by day and beatboxer by night (I have heard her, and she is brilliant at it!). At one time, I would have assumed these 20-somethings to be quirky exceptions to the rule. But it feels like they are no longer such outliers.

"Here are some of the things that struck me about the way they see the world – and their place in it.

"College isn't just a degree. For this group of Gen Z, college is not just the route to a job – instead, it's a space for opportunities. They aren't fixated on the classes they take or the tests, or even the curriculum. College, for them, is a springboard for networking and experimenting. It's where they can mull over or even launch an early version of a start-up or do multiple internships without any financial burden.

"India's Gen Z look for new opportunities at university. They won't jump to find a job. Young Indians typically never took a "gap year" between high school and college. Taking an entire year off was seen as self-indulgent or a wasteful luxury. But the 18-year-olds that I speak to say they don't want to waste their life trying to be someone they are not. So, they prefer taking a few months or a year to figure out who they are before they set out to pursue their goals. They want to marry late, if at all. Nearly every 20-something I have spoken to sees commitment as a trap. They want to avoid it early in their life. For them, knowing themselves and owning themselves is far more important than someone else holding their hand.

"They will take financial risks. Although most of them grew up watching their parents focused on stability, they seem to realise that it's a different time now – inequality is wider, dreams are bigger and the paths to success are many.

For them, money is not a source of survival but a source of freedom.

A bungalow in a posh neighbourhood isn't the goal. Rather, it's having money to splurge on a pair of Air Jordans after investing monthly savings in stocks and crypto.

"Many young Indians see social media as their school. Social media is for learning. YouTube is their school. They don't particularly care where the lessons are happening. They follow the right people on Instagram for quick and consumable nuggets of wisdom. They have ambition and audacity. And they have one quality that sets them apart from every previous generation in India – a genuine appetite for risk.

"Risk has always been a four-letter word in middle class India.

Even in my parents' generation, stability was key. Work-life balance, career fulfilment, impact – these were terms thrown around by the privileged elite.

But Gen Z is not just aware of global opportunities that are available to them – they are also not shying away from giving it a shot. They know that there is a path to retire at 35 – and they are not embarrassed to chase it – as opposed to slogging until you are 60.

"It's why the flamboyant founders of successful start-ups – Vijay Shekhar Sharma of digital payments platform Paytm or Ritesh Agarwal, who became India's youngest billionaire when he founded India's largest hotel network – have become icons.

"Young entrepreneurs like Ritesh Agarwal inspire Indians The fact that Paytm makes no profit, or that Oyo is struggling under a mountain of debt which fuelled its rapid expansion, is not an immediate concern.

"And that worries me. Growing up, we were made to wait, often against our choice. We stood in line to buy milk, waited for hours to call someone or days for a letter to be delivered. We waited years to buy a vehicle and a lifetime to find financial stability. Patience was learnt not by choice, but by the design of the India we lived in. Now, everything we need – food, clothes, books, movies, even relationships – is available a click away. The pace of the world, combined with Gen Z's ambition, makes them want everything now – I saw a tweet recently that read: "My problem is I want everything today."

"This is the case with Gen Z everywhere – but in India, our economy is at odds with this generation's ambition. Will the young accountant become a full-time beatboxer? Will the 20-something artist find a job at a graphic design firm?

Can this restless generation bridge the gap between aspirations and options, or will it fall into the chasm in between?

Only time will tell."

Ankur Warikoo is an Indian entrepreneur, a bestselling author, teacher and content creator.

Although the people of India are guaranteed the right to worship how they feel, during the past few years, in some parts of the country Christians have come into various decrees of persecution mainly from Hindus. Some parts of India are definitely not safe for Christians to live openly. During my last visit I was taken to the site of several churches that had been burnt to the ground by extremists. But we know that the church is continues to grow despite the persecution. 4/2/2025 India (International Christian Concern) — The Evangelical Fellowship of India's Religious Liberty Commission

(EFIRLC) verified 640 incidents of violence and discrimination against Christians in India in 2024, which is more than quadruple the 147 cases recorded in 2014.

Murray Noble of Open Doors, Australia has written: "While persecution is oppressive in many countries. India is definitely not a safe place for Christians to live openly in many parts of the country." Without going into distressing details, Noble says Open Doors Australia receives reports of violent acts of persecution in India almost every day.

The modern day phenomena of the India diaspora is having an astonishing effect on the world. According to the Ministry of External Affairs the report updated on 26 November 2024, stated there are 35.4 million non-resident Indians (NRIs) and People of Indian Origins (PIOs) (including OCIs) residing outside India. They comprise the world's largest overseas diaspora. Every year, 2.5 million (25 lakh) Indians immigrate overseas, making India the nation with the highest annual number of emigrants in the world. (*Wikipedia.*)

The Indian diaspora in New Zealand is a diverse community of around 300,000 people with a variety of cultural traditions, languages, and religions. They are active and influential in many areas of society, including business and community initiatives.

Here are some facts about the Indian population in New Zealand:

> The first recorded Indian in New Zealand was Mamouth Cassem, who was born in Pondicherry around 1755. The 1881 census recorded only six Indians in New Zealand.
>
> The 2023 census recorded 292,092 people who claimed Indian descent, making it the third-largest ethnic group in the country and their language Hindi is the fifth most spoken language in New Zealand. 65% of them live in Auckland.
>
> The median income of Indian adults in New Zealand is higher than the median income for the country's overall population. An Indian community association estimates that people of Indian origin contribute more than NZ $10 billion to New Zealand's GDP.
>
> *Wikipedia.*

I can leave my apartment in Central Auckland and see that right next door is an excellent convenience shop owned by a Punjabi family. Right next to that is an eatery serving inexpensive but good quality Indian food. Next door is a liquor store owned by a man from Gujarat, Vas Vyas, (whose wife is the manager of a prominent NZ frozen foods company). He sells a full range of wines and spirits. Next is a small café providing takeaway lunches, next door is an Indian-owned Vape shop owned by a South Indian. On the other side in the adjacent building is a full scale Indian restaurant, plus a coffee shop. Across the road is a convenience store is a that is truly convenient in that it has a huge range of items and services run by Meena Patel of Gujarat.

I've sold my car due to parking problems in the central city so I often need a taxi or an Uber or Didi. The driver is likely to be an Indian. My destination is a sleep clinic where the doctor is a Punjabi and whose nurse is Tamil along with the receptionist who is her sister. My return home is in an Uber, the driver being an Marathi civil engineer. I joked with him saying that I hoped he didn't learn to drive in a Bombay taxi. "Oh no sir, there I'd only get two or three fares a day but here it is work all day.'

As I come to the conclusion of this book, I cannot help but think of the huge problems the country faces. Think of the way the climate of the world seems to be changing. This photo here depicts a family saved from the terror of the huge cyclone named Odisha that struck on 25th October 1999. The Bible Society sent a team to help and as I was in the country at the time, I joined them. This was the most intense tropical cyclone ever recorded in the North Indian Ocean. Winds of 160mph (200kph) swept everything aside. It was the most heart-breaking experience to see what it did to the country. Property was destroyed on such a huge scale damaging or destroying 1,600,000 homes. And killed 9,887 people.

We see this family standing before a makeshift shelter, still coming to terms with their misfortune but so grateful their lives were spared. Government officials were able to warn the people to flee inland. One of the most uncomfortable nights I have ever had was when visiting the site of this cyclone, I slept on top of medical supplies that were packed almost to the roof of a still-standing warehouse – supplies that had been provided by UNESCO but still remained undelivered. It was not that it was uncomfortable sleeping on cartons of hypodermic syringes and all kinds of medicines, but the thoughts of all those people suffering from the aftermath of this tragedy. Later I learned that my own little country had given $99,823 to the relief fund. The government flew in nearly a thousand people from neighbouring states who were of the caste that could handle dead bodies.

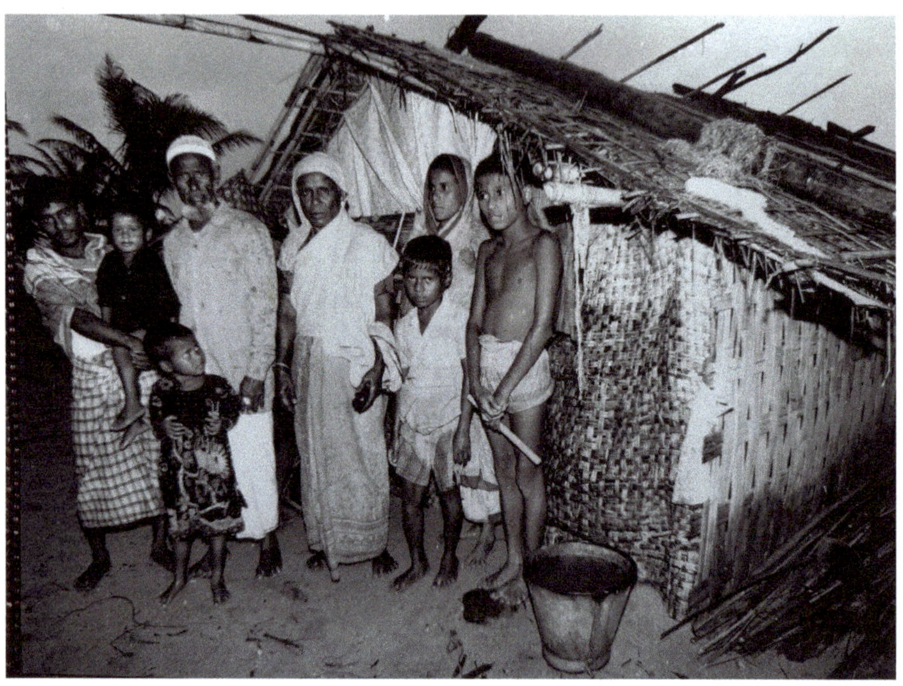

CONCLUSION

I was a schoolboy, aged 12, when I heard the news that India had become an independent country. Returning missionaries had meetings at our church and told of this momentous event. They showed amateur movies of the celebrations. I remember nothing of what they said about it, expect that the many Christians there have a role to play in moving the country forward. But as I grew and learned about the multiplicity and difficulty of learning the languages, I resolved as a young Christian, that if the Lord wanted me to be a missionary, then let it not be to India! The first of many missionaries from New Zealand to go to India was Emily Starck in 1904. China was the other place I didn't want to go to! But I did eventually live in Hong Kong for ten years!

The country continues to advance. India's 1.46 billion people now lead in technical innovation: the spiritual quest I witnessed in 1960 persists, blending ancient faith with modern aspirations. As a Christian, I am interested to note that people of my faith are now 2.5% of the population and number 35 million and growing fast.

I'll be up to date and quote Chat GPT:

> India's economic outlook for 2025 is strong, with the International Monetary Fund (IMF) forecasting a 6.4% growth rate, positioning it as the fastest-growing major economy globally. This growth is supported by strong domestic demand, government investment in infrastructure, and resilience to global economic headwinds. Key sectors like pharmaceuticals, healthcare, infrastructure, and consumer goods are expected to drive performance, benefiting from robust exports and a growing middle class.

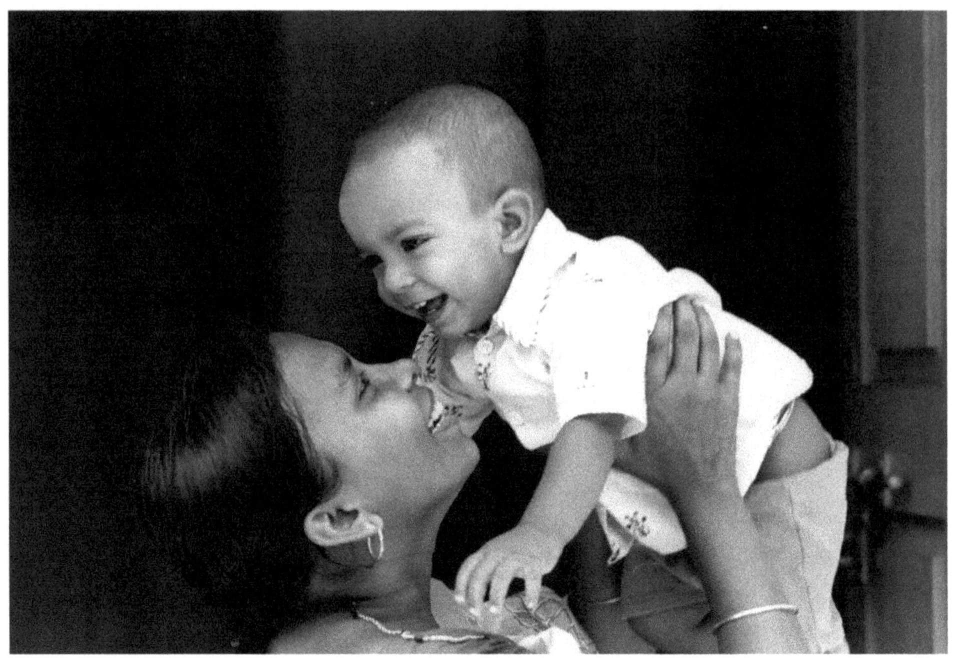

Hindi-speaking mother and child.

Let me finish by repeating an opening paragraph of this book:

> The most important thing to understand about India is its complexity. "There never was a land so riddled by inconsistency, so defiant of generalisation, so bewilderingly varied, or so preposterously loaded with idiosyncrasies. It is doubtful whether anyone has ever understood more than a few parts of it well, and none, certainly, can have comprehended it all, for the full range of India is too wide and too elusive and too detailed to grasp."

BIBLIOGRAPHY

David Abram, India, *The Rough Guide*. The Rough Guides

Geoff Crowther, *India a travel survival kit*, Lonely Planet

Gregory David Roberts, *Shantaram*. Picador

Gurcharan Das, *India Unbound*. Penguimn

Khajuraho Guide, Tilak Printing Press

Christopher Kremer, *Inhaling the Mahatma*. Harper Collins

Lal Chand, *India Guide*, Lal Ch & Sons

Lawrence James, *Raj*. Little, Brown and Company

Maria Raffaella Fiory Ceccopieri, *India*. Touring Club Italiano

McKim Marriot, *Village India*. University of Chicago Press

Paul C Pet, Geoffrey Moorhouse, Brian Hollingsworth, *Rail Across India*. Abbeville Press

Suketu Mehta, *Maximum City*, Review

Colleen Redit, *Realising a Vision Through Faith*. Christian Missions Charitable Trust

Robert Young Pelton, *The World's Most Dangerous Places*. Collins

William Dalrymple, *White Mughals*. Flamingo

William Dalrymple, *The Golden Road*. Bloomsbury

APPENDIX

COUNTRIES, TERRITORIES AND DISPUTED TERRITORIES VISITED BY THE AUTHOR – where I usually found a few people from India.

There seems to be no official list of countries of the world, in fact I have found no two lists the same. Many travellers base their count on geography, political state either at the time of visit or later, or whether it issues its own postage stamps or currency. This one doesn't include airports!

We could also add Kashmir (162).

AFRICA

Angola
Benin
Burkina Faso
Burundi
Cameroon
Central African Republic
Chad
Congo-Kinshasa
Cote d'Ivoire
Congo-Brazzaville
Egypt
Equatorial Guinea
Eritrea
Ethiopia
Ghana
Kenya
Letsos
Madagascar
Malawi
Mali
Mozambique
Namibia
Niger
Nigeria
Rwanda
Seychelles
South Africa
South Sudan
Sudan
Swaziland
Tanzania
Transkei
Togo
Uganda
Zanzibar
Zambia
Zimbabwe

ASIA AND MIDDLE EAST

Armenia
Bahrain
Bangladesh
Brunei
Cambodia
China
Hong Kong
Gaza Strip
India
Indonesia
Israel
Japan
Jordan
Kazakhstan
North Korea
South Korea
Laos
Lebanon
Malaysia
Macau
Mauritius
Mongolia
Myanmar
Nepal
Oman
Pakistan
Palestinian West Bank
Philippines
Singapore
Sri Lanka

Syria
Taiwan
Thailand
Timor Leste
Turkey
Uzbekistan
Vietnam

PACIFIC

American Samoa
Australia
Cook Islands
Fiji
French Polynesia
Kiribati
Nauru
New Caledonia
New Zealand
Niue
Papua New Guinea
Solomon Islands
Tonga
Tuvalu
Vanuatu
Western Samoa

AMERICAS

Argentina
Aruba
Barbados
Bolivia
Brazil
Canada
Chile
Colombia
Cuba
Curacao
Dominican Republic
Ecuador
El Salvador
Honduras
Guatemala
Haiti
Jamaica
Mexico
Netherlands Antilles
Nicaragua
Panama
Paraguay
Peru
St Vincent and the Grenadines
Trinidad & Tobago
Uruguay
United States of America
Venezuela

EUROPE

Albania
Austria
Belarus
Belgium
Bosnia-Herzegovina
Bulgaria
Czech Republic
Denmark
Croatia
East Germany
Estonia
England
Finland
France
Germany
Georgia
Greece
Holy See
Hungary
Ireland
Italy
Latvia
Liechtenstein
Lithuania
Luxembourg
Moldova
Monaco
Netherlands
Northern Ireland
Norway
Poland
Portugal
Romania
Russia
Scotland
Slovakia
Slovenia
Spain
Switzerland
Turkey
Ukraine
Wales